NATIONAL CITY PUBLIC LIBRARY

3 3835 00022 5672

D0603556

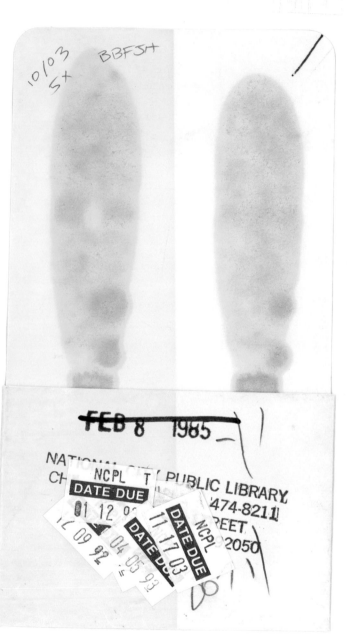

10/03
SX   BBFSH

FEB 8 1985

NATIONAL CITY PUBLIC LIBRARY
CH...   474-8211
...REET
...2050

NCPL
DATE DUE
01 12 03

04 05 93

NCPL
DATE DUE
11 17 03

National City Public Library
200 East 12th Street
National City, California 92050

National City, Public Library
200 East 12th Street,
National City, California 92050

The Young Writer's Handbook

National City Public Library
200 East 12th Street
National City, California 92050

National City Public Library
200 East 12th Street
National City, California 92050

FEB 8 1985

THIS BOOK IS THE PROPERTY OF
THE NATIONAL CITY PUBLIC LIBRARY

The Young Writer's Handbook

Susan and Stephen Tchudi

Charles Scribner's Sons/New York

THIS BOOK IS THE PROPERTY OF
THE NATIONAL CITY PUBLIC LIBRARY

FEB 8 1985

Byrd Baylor, "The way to make a song . . ." from *The Way to Start a Day*. Copyright © 1976, 1977 Byrd Baylor. Reprinted with the permission of Charles Scribner's Sons.

Millicent Brower, "down by the brook," in *The Scribner Anthology for Young People*, edited by Anne Diven. Copyright © 1976 Charles Scribner's Sons. Reprinted with the permission of Charles Scribner's Sons.

Diane Rodgers, "Proofreader's Plea," reprinted from *Writer's Digest*, December 1982. Reprinted with the permission of Diane Rodgers.

Copyright © 1984 Susan and Stephen Tchudi

Library of Congress Cataloging in Publication Data
Tchudi, Susan J. (Susan Jane), date
The young writer's handbook.
Includes index.
  Summary: Suggests helpful procedures and approaches for the beginning writer in areas of interest such as the journal, letter writing, creative writing, school reports, topics and experiments, editing, and publishing.
  1. English language—Composition and exercises—Juvenile literature. 2. Authorship—Juvenile literature. [1. English language—Composition and exercises. 2. Authorship. 3. Creative writing. 4. Report writing. 5. Letter writing] I. Tchudi, Stephen, date. II. Title.
PE1408.T36 1984   808'.042   84-5312
ISBN 0-684-18090-1

This book published simultaneously in the United States of America and in Canada—Copyright under the Berne Convention
All rights reserved. No part of this book may be reproduced in any form without the permission of Charles Scribner's Sons.

1 3 5 7 9 11 13 15 17 19 F/C 20 18 16 14 12 10 8 6 4 2

Printed in the United States of America

Contents

Preface

For almost two decades we have been working with young writers in Michigan and other states, conducting workshops, teaching classes, judging contests, helping to organize readings and literary magazines. The term "young" is not meant to put down novice writers or to remind them of their youth. Rather, we see it as a term that emphasizes opportunity and accomplishment, for *young* writers have almost an entire lifetime of scrawling and scribbling and typing and revising and publishing ahead of them, and we're envious of that.

One of the things we've discovered about young writers is their interest in doing more writing than is customarily required of them in school. When folks sign up for our workshops and classes it's because they have a hankering to put pen to paper more often than they do now. We have written this book for people like that, and we frankly hope that among the "young" readers of this book will be some adults who've always had that urge to write but haven't been able to do much about it.

Whether you're eight or eighty, then, we hope you will find *The Young Writer's Handbook* helpful.

As you'll learn in Chapter One and elsewhere, we believe that one person cannot actually teach others to write, if by "teach" you mean "tell exactly how to do it." Experienced writers can offer a great many tips and pointers that will be helpful to the young writer (and we have included quotations from a great many writers in the book for just that reason), but we also believe, along with thousands and thousands of other writers, that:

One learns to write by writing.

In general, the more writing you do, the better you'll become at it.

The Young Writer's Handbook, then, is an idea book and guide, not a "how to" book in the strictest sense. We'll toss out hundreds of ideas we think you may enjoy exploring in language (drawing on our experience in those young writers' workshops), and we'll suggest some procedures and approaches that we think you'll find helpful. In the end, however, you will use this book to teach yourself to write, something we believe you will find enormously satisfying.

There are only two chapters of the book that we suggest you should read in order: One and Two. These discuss some basic questions and issues: "Why Write?" and "Finding an Approach to Writing." After that, you may want to skip about, reading the chapters that address themselves to your particular needs and interests. In Chapter Three we present the idea of the writing journal as a place to gather ideas, impressions, bits of language, perceptions. In Chapter Four we will help you come up with dozens of writing topics that you can write about successfully. Chapter Five describes letter writing and all the things you can accomplish with a sheet of paper, an envelope, and a stamp. Six tells about so-called creative or imaginative writing—poetry, fiction, drama—with suggestions on how to use your experience as a basis for writing your own "literature." In Chapter Seven we discuss school writing and how to use your writing skills to get better results in school. Chapter Eight describes how you can use your community—whether a large city or a small town—as a source of rich and interesting writing experiments. In Chapter Nine we discuss editing—how to correct and improve your writing—and in Chapter Ten we describe some ways in which you can find wider audiences for your writing and—who knows?—maybe even make a few bucks by selling your writing or winning contests or scholarships.

Whether you are writing just for the fun of it, to explore your world, to impress your teachers, or to become a published author, we hope you find the process a satisfying one, something that opens the world to you and helps you learn something about who you are—which is, perhaps, the most significant task of your life.

Okemos, Michigan
Virginia Beach, Virginia
Martha's Vineyard, Massachusetts
Summer 1983

The Young Writer's Handbook

Why Write?

1

The Canadian writer and media critic, Marshall McLuhan, has intrigued and provoked writers and nonwriters alike by declaring, "Print is dead."° In our time, he said, electronic forms of communication—especially television—have made print and writing far less useful and important than they once were. He predicted that in the future people will rely on electronic forms of communication more and more, with the possibility that books and newspapers and magazines as we know them will disappear before the end of this century.

If Marshall McLuhan is right, the question that heads this chapter is especially important: Why write? Why learn and practice a skill that is obsolete or that will be "antique" before you reach middle age?

We believe that Marshall McLuhan was exaggerating when he made his statement, saying something extreme to make a point and to encourage people to think about the future. If we thought print were dead or dying, we wouldn't have written this book (and we wouldn't be writers at all). However, before we plunge into talking (or writing) about writing, we think it might be useful for you to think about the role that writing has played in human civilization in the past, the role it plays in your life today, and the role it may play in your future.

°Marshall McLuhan, *Understanding Media: The Extensions of Man* (1965).

The Development of Writing

Much of what we know about the history of humankind has come to us through writing. Indeed, most of what we know about human life prior to writing—prior to "written history"—is based on speculation and guesswork. For thousands of years, people have used writing to make records of their lives: They have written laws and treaties to maintain order and peace; they have made written agreements for trading goods and kept records of commerce; they have written down records of seasons, crops, plantings, and harvests; they have observed and written explanations of natural phenomena like day and night, winter and summer, water and earth, moons and stars, animals and plants; they have used writing to try to understand spiritual life and to create religions; they have written myths and legends to describe their views of the world; they have created educational books to teach their young; and they have written about their experiences and emotions in poetry, drama, song, and story. Throughout the ages people have used written language to enhance their existence, to explain themselves, and to understand themselves and their world.

Primitive people—those who lived about 20,000 years ago—used "writing" in the form of pictures. Evidence has been found that earliest humans made markings on cave walls, on stones, and on objects to denote ownership or to represent religious beliefs or experiences. However, these drawings were a far cry from writing as we know it.

The pictures and markings made about 5,000 years ago seemed to tell some sort of story or show connections among events in people's lives. The drawings became symbols, representing more than just a single object. These *pictograms* (or stories told through pictures) have been discovered throughout the world, carved or written on stone, shells, tree bark, and animal skins. Early stories told through pictograms, such as animals and hunters, seemingly in chase, reflected people's relationships with their environment. Still, these drawings were not true writing.

Somewhere around 3000–2000 B.C. the use of *ideograms* developed.

People needed and wanted to express more in writing than they could with simple pictures. Ideograms are symbols in which a rough sketch, say, of the sun, could represent not just a single object—the sun itself—but several related ideas: day, good weather, the east (that place or direction where the sun rose). Soon ideograms could express ideas and emotions, not just actions, objects, or events. The ideogram of an eye with a tear, for example, was a symbol for sorrow in cultures as different as the Mayas and Aztecs in what is now Central America and the Chinese in the Orient.

The next stage in the development of writing seems to have taken place in western Asia and around the Mediterranean Sea, where some of the early great cultures flourished: Sumeria, Mesopotamia, Phoenicia, Egypt, Rome, and Greece. As these cultures came into contact with one another, they needed to find common systems of communication, including writing.

The *cuneiform* system—developed in Sumeria (now Iraq) around 3500 B.C. and adopted by many ancient civilizations in that area—used marks made by pressing a wedge-shaped stylus or marking tool in wet clay. At first, the cuneiform markings represented objects, actions, and ideas as ideograms, but gradually the marks became "streamlined," looking less and less like "the real thing." At the same time those symbols stamped in wet clay came to represent or stand for specific words in the spoken language. Egyptian *hieroglyphics* are another example of drawings gradually simplified and coming to stand for whole words in the language. At this point in history, writing was rather close to what we conceive it to be, but one thing was missing: the alphabet.

This development took place in Phoenicia, a neighbor of both Greece and Rome, which was known for its manufacturing and trading throughout the Mediterranean and was a powerful influence in the development of Western culture. The Phoenicians adapted earlier writing systems, using marks to represent not whole words, but individual sounds in their language. This may seem rather simple or obvious to us, but it was an ingenious and remarkable achievement. Through letter-symbols, the Phoenicians could use just a few symbols, about two dozen, in place of thousands and thousands of cuneiform symbols or hieroglyphics. (You may know that written Chinese has never made this transition. Thus, learning to write Chinese is very difficult, and writers spend much of their lifetime learning to master tens of thousands of separate character or word drawings.)

The modification of the alphabet to the point at which we can recognize the letters came through the Greeks and the Romans. The Greeks, who had contact with the Phoenicians through trade, borrowed their alphabet, adopting nineteen of their twenty-two symbols and adding some of their own to create a twenty-four letter alphabet, beginning with the characters named *alpha* and *beta* that give us our word *alphabet*. The Romans— neighbors and successors of the Greeks as the major world power—took that basic system of alphabetic writing and carried it through their part of the world as the written form of their language, Latin. For centuries the Romans dominated a large part of the world, and they left behind legacies of government, religion, language, and, of course, *writing*.

Along with the development of the alphabet, the "technology" of writing has steadily improved, making the use of writing and print more available to everyone. For the caveman who drew on walls, "writing" was slow and laborious and the writer had to depend upon someone walking by to examine his work. In the cuneiform system, printing on a clay tablet with a stylus, writing was faster and somewhat more portable, but still very slow and cumbersome. In Egypt, written language was at first used only by the priests, who had the materials and the slave labor to create writing, but later the Egyptians pioneered in developing better and lighter writing materials: papyrus, parchment, and vellum. On the other side of the globe, the Chinese developed paper about the first century A.D. When paper began to be used in Europe several centuries later, writing became much less expensive and more available to the people. Still, in the Middle Ages, books and manuscripts were rare and expensive, most of them having been created and owned by the Church, whose scribes spent lifetimes copying.

You probably know of Johann Gutenberg, who is generally credited with inventing "movable type" that made printing practicable. From Guten-

Figure 1 *The Evolution of the Letters M and H from Pictograms*

berg's time on, there has been immense interest in our culture in letting every person learn to read and write. The United States has one of the highest literacy rates in the world. We value writing and reading so much that the acquisition of these skills is an absolutely central part of our educational system.

The story of the evolution of both the alphabet and writing materials shows how important writing is and has become to people. The entire course of civilization can be traced in and through writing. People's needs to organize, control, and understand their worlds have been inextricably tied to writing, providing ways to order and comprehend and define. That need has not diminished in our electronic age.

The Uses of Writing Today

Despite the development of sophisticated telecommunications systems and the widespread use of computers, much of the work (and fun) of the world is done through the written word. The laws of the land, their interpretation, and their enforcement are maintained through print. Agreements between nations on war and peace, commerce, and ecology are written and signed. Businesses and industries may need their phones and computers, but their work could not go on without the written word, and many business people worry about the "paper avalanche" that is created in their offices every day. Proposals for new products and services are developed, submitted, and approved in writing. Production, evaluation, and distribution depend on the writing and implementing of a plan. Scientists, doctors, and social scientists—people working on the problems in our lives—must have pen and paper handy to record their hypotheses and experiments and observations.

There are writers who interpret and explain the world for us: journalists, who report events of the world and new developments in education, science, medicine, art, politics, and religion; historians, philosophers, and social analysts, who give their opinions about the meaning of what's happening to us; authors of poems and plays and stories, who interpret experience in their own way through writing; reviewers, who give us their opinions of how successful things are in our world.

Many people write for small or private audiences. Even though the phone company advertises that telephones are personal and efficient, many of us prefer to keep in touch through letters. Many people keep journals and diaries that are meant for their eyes only. Most of us feel a need to keep a pen and a pad of paper handy for notes and scribbles, sometimes to ourselves, sometimes to others.

Is print dead? Not by a long shot.

The Future of Writing

We think it likely that in your lifetime you will see some remarkable changes in the way print is created, packaged, and distributed. For instance, your daily paper may soon not be printed on paper at all, but will arrive on your television screen. Instead of checking out a book at a library, you may someday borrow a computer or video disk that will display the text on a screen. Instead of writing with pen and ink on paper, you will certainly learn to use an electronic word processor, and you may even come to own a small portable word processor that you can carry around with you and type ideas into whenever you want. It is even conceivable that in your lifetime the alphabet itself may change as new letters and symbols, more suitable for use in computers and other electronic devices, come to stand alongside and then replace the letters developed so long ago by the Greeks and Romans.

However, the *word*—language—is here to stay. No matter what alphabet and what language develop, there will still be a need for *writers*—people who write in language—on the face of this planet.

Why Do People Write?

Just about everyone writes. However, some people become *writers*, those who enjoy writing for its own sake, who write for fun or profit. Many people become writers by chance. They never intended to become writers or thought of themselves as writers, but suddenly they became involved in a job in which they needed to write. Many of these people felt they had no particular skills or abilities in writing until they were in a situation in which they had to write. They learned to write by writing, by getting responses from people around them, and through reading. Somewhere in the process, they became *writers*.

Others have recognized their interest and ability early in life and have chosen writing as a profession or hobby. Often lawyers and journalists feel comfortable with their language skills and choose their professions to make use of their strengths. Still others write for personal satisfaction and find it growing into a career.

Barbara Wersba, a young adult novelist, says that

> . . . many writers, if you read what they say about themselves, say they write a book to find out what they think. I write a book to find out who I am. It's a process of awakening; one of the richest ways of finding out who you are.°

Paul Zindel, a Pulitzer Prize–winning playwright and another young adult novelist, also uses his writing in this way. He says that when he begins to write,

> I'm solving a problem for myself. The writing of the story acts in much the same way that a dream functions, bringing one as close as one can come to a solution to a problem that's posed.†

°Paul Janeczko, "An Interview with Barbara Wersba," *The English Journal* (November 1976).
†Paul Janeczko, "An Interview with Paul Zindel," *The English Journal* (October 1977).

Novelist Judith Guest writes to master her experiences:

> ... it's a feeling of "I'm going to set up this situation and I'm going to make it turn out the way I want it to turn out in real life."*

For some people, writing becomes a way of life. Robert Cormier has worked as a journalist by day and a novelist by night and follows the "routine of writing constantly":

> I go to work every day and I actively write there. It's woven into the fabric of my existence. . . . I just continually write, continually absorb impressions, emotions.†

Paul Zindel emphasizes that the "true writer" writes to satisfy himself and because he has to; he is not "someone who becomes a writer through technique or artifice, or to make money."‡

Few of us have the leisure to devote our entire lives to writing. It is almost axiomatic among writers that one needs to have a regular paying job in order to support the habit of writing, even if that writing produces some income. Chances are, however, that whether or not you choose a career in writing, you fit the definition of the true writer who writes out of a desire—even a compulsion—to write. You write to satisfy yourself, and so, it might be added, do we.

Writing in Your World

We've talked a bit about writing—past, present, future—and about writers' views of their work. Now we'd like you to focus on the written word in your own life. Since language is the tool of the writer's trade, seeing how language touches your life and affects your thinking and feeling will help

---

*Paul Janeczko, "An Interview with Judith Guest," *The English Journal* (March 1978).
†Paul Janeczko, "An Interview with Robert Cormier," *The English Journal* (September 1977).
‡"An Interview with Paul Zindel."

you discover the ways in which you want to develop your own writing and the directions your writing will take.

Begin by making a collection of the ways in which you encounter language in your life. Where do you see words and print every day? How do you use spoken as well as written language? You might even try to categorize the *types* of language you encounter. For example, think of all the people you talk to and who talk to you during a day. Think of contacts with parents, other family members, teachers (school, music, art, church), coaches, store clerks, friends and members of their families, and so on. Note the things they talk about and how their personalities and moods affect their language. If you know people who once lived in other parts of the country, pay attention to how their language is different from your own. Write down ways of talking that you find interesting or amusing. Become a collector of snatches and snippets of conversation, attuning your ear to listen to others' unique uses of language.

Pay attention, too, to the language you hear on television and the radio. Compare the language you hear on various kinds of shows: children's programs, news programs, situation comedies, serious drama, soaps, documentaries, variety or musical shows, game shows, and human interest programs. Notice what seems to be common to the language used and then see what seems unusual or unique. Listen to the language of advertising, which is often bright, glittery, and catchy. Collect slogans, which, in our fast-paced society, are used to attract people's attention and persuade them of the validity of an idea.

Read over the family newspaper for examples of diverse language: news, features, reviews, interviews, editorials, opinion columns, features for children, letters to the editor, sports, horoscopes, news analyses. Look over the headlines to see how the reader's eye is drawn to particular stories. Write down the examples—good and bad—of language you encounter in the paper.

Examine the magazines you and your family read. What kinds of stories and articles do you find there? Compare different kinds of magazines for:

homemakers, working mothers, mechanics buffs, computer addicts, moviegoers, dancers, knitters, weavers, woodworkers, dog/cat/horse owners, vacationers, the fashion conscious, game players, television watchers. (You won't have all those magazines available in your own home, of course; go to your local library to see the wide range that is available to people with special interests.) Again, study how the language and style change for particular audiences. How do computer or cat or movie fanciers talk to one another?

Notice how magazine language differs from that of your school books. Think about the style and form used in texts as compared to that in magazines and newspapers. Collect examples of interesting and entertaining language in your school reading.

After you have spent some time exploring language in your daily life—both the language you hear and the language you read—spend some time thinking about your pleasure reading. Do you prefer to read stories? plays? poems? novels? What is your favorite subject? Who are your preferred authors? What is your all-time favorite book? Do you have favorite quotes or sections of special books? What books do you like to read again and again? Then think about why your favorites are your favorites. What in the language and content appeals to you? What do you like about the characters or situations?

Finally, think about the writing you do in your life from morning until night. What kind of writing do you do for school? Do you write letters to family or friends? Do you keep a journal or diary? Do you write down observations of things that you see or things you are doing? Do you write notes and reminders to yourself? Do you write plays, poems, or stories on your own?

Now think about what you would like to accomplish with your writing. Why did you pick up this book? Where did your interest in writing come from? Perhaps your teacher thinks you have a flair for writing and suggested that you do more on your own. Or perhaps a relative loved an article you published in the school paper and said you ought to become a writer.

Maybe you want to improve your school writing and prepare yourself for the next (and some say harder) grade. Perhaps you have hopes of being a journalist or magazine editor in the future and you'd like to get started now. Possibly you want to get a position on the school paper next year and are sharpening your skills in preparation. Maybe you've decided that your poems and plays are good, but not good enough, and you feel ready to move on to new levels of achievement.

Take a few minutes to list your goals for yourself as a writer. Try to be specific about the things you want to accomplish as you work on your writing or as you use this book. The clearer you can be, the more helpful the book can be in answering your questions.

Learning to write is not an easy process, but it can be a very satisfying one. Don't expect to be able to master the craft immediately. Learning to write takes time and practice, and many, many professional writers say that they feel like learners at the trade of writing all their lives. When you are working on accomplishing something, you may sometimes lose sight of other parts of your writing. If you develop a critical eye, you'll always be able to see new things to try in writing. In short, be patient, and give it time.

Judith Guest, again, says this to young writers:

My advice would be to write and write and try to keep thinking positively about . . . writing. In other words, don't waste a lot of energy putting down what you're doing.°

Paul Zindel agrees that writing is a learn-by-doing skill and art:

I think . . . young people interested in writing must simply *do*. They must sit down and write as much as they can about whatever they feel they should.†

°"An Interview with Judith Guest."
†"An Interview with Paul Zindel."

Author Mary Stolz stresses your own reading and writing as the best way to learn:

> Children write to me and say, "I'd like to be an author. What shall I do?" I have a reply I always make, and fear they think I have some recipe that I'm too grudging to give them. I tell them, "Read a lot and write a lot, read a lot and write a lot."[*]

Writing is more than just practice, however; it involves your whole self—your thoughts, your attitudes, your feelings and experiences. The writer must see things clearly and recreate those things for others to understand and appreciate. Barbara Wersba believes that writing is a process of

> . . . unlearning all the prejudices and conventional ideas that we're taught when we're young. To be a writer you have to see the world for the first time and pretend you know nothing about it. You have to stay very fresh and open.

She adds:

> The most important thing for a writer is to learn who he is.[†]

---

[*]Paul Janeczko, "An Interview with Mary Stolz," *The English Journal* (October 1975).
[†]"An Interview with Barbara Wersba."

Finding an Approach
to Writing

2

To be a writer, you have to write. Perhaps that sounds too obvious, but there are many people who go around with "great ideas" they "intend" to write—stories, memoirs, poems they have "in their heads"—that they never get on paper. It takes more than creative thoughts and good ideas to be a writer. You have to get your ideas from your mind to the page. To help you do this, you need to find your own approach to writing: the times and places, even the tools and habits, that enable you to write most easily.

A Time and Place to Write

The best way to get yourself writing is to set up a regular routine or schedule to follow. If you can, try to find a time every day in which you can write (or maybe four days out of five or every weekday). Some people put off writing until they have a big block of time—like a weekend or vacation—to begin. Others say they can only write when they are "inspired." Most professional writers, however, reject those approaches. Writing, they say, requires disciplined work. Novelist Nathaniel Benchley puts in a schedule that's typical of many writers:

> I write every morning. I see if I can get a thousand words down. Every morning, summer and winter, seven days a week.*

---

*Paul Janeczko, "An Interview with Nathaniel Benchley," *The English Journal* (September 1976).

14

Humorist, novelist, filmmaker Woody Allen once observed that if you simply write one page a day, at the end of a year you will have 365 pages, and that's a book!°

It will also help you to set a specific time of day when you will do your writing. Most professional writers seem to prefer the morning, because that is when they are freshest and most energetic. Paul Zindel says he is

> . . . definitely a morning person. I like to work between eight and noon. Three hours is plenty and I'm exhausted by that time.†

When you are going to school, it might be hard to find time in the morning to get your writing done. However, if you're a morning person and do your most creative work then, it might be worth the effort for you to get up a half hour earlier to do your writing.

There's nothing magic about morning, however, and there are plenty of writers who are "night people." Two of our friends who are poets wait until everyone in their families has gone to bed, then write in the wee hours of the morning, while all is quiet. We don't recommend that for a school-going young writer, but you get the idea: You have to find a time when you can get your writing done steadily and efficiently, without distraction. It may be that your best time will be a half hour or hour after school, after dinner, or right before bed. Of course, if you are lucky enough to get inspiration at another time, write then. And if your "regular time" is occupied, don't let that be an excuse for not writing. Most writers are flexible enough to be able to change their routine from time to time.

Find a place where it is comfortable to write. Perhaps you are one of those people who can write *anywhere*—riding the bus, watching television, eating in the school lunchroom, listening to your teacher give instructions, babysitting. However, many writers like to do their writing in a special place. Some like to work sitting at a desk in a straight-backed chair; some

---

°Woody Allen, *Without Feathers* (1974).
†Paul Janeczko, "An Interview with Paul Zindel," *The English Journal* (October 1977).

like to curl up on the couch or in a comfortable chair; some like to get away from home and write in a special place like the library or a snack shop. Some can write in the midst of hubbub; others must have it quiet. It's good, too, to be flexible here. Novelist/journalist Robert Cormier has nurtured his flexibility:

> I do a lot of writing at night when everyone's asleep and it's quiet. But I do not require quiet. . . . my training on the newspaper has helped me, you know, with the phones ringing, people coming and going, writing for a deadline.°

The Tools of the Trade

Though you may develop the skill of writing in chaos, with people coming and going, with phones ringing, you may still want to have your own writing nook or cranny, a place where you can keep all your work, all the materials you need, a place where you do your serious writing. You might have a desk in your room where you can store "the tools of the trade": paper, pencils, drafts, completed copies. If you don't have a desk, you might store your writing materials in a cardboard box that you've covered with contact paper for decoration (or just a plain cardboard box that you keep in your closet).

Of course, one good thing about writing is that you don't need very many special "tools"; a pencil and some paper are enough to get you started. However, the writing process might be made easier and more enjoyable if you have your own, personal equipment:

Pens and Pencils. Some writers find they can do their best writing with a certain pen or pencil. Some only use ball-point pens, some prefer felt-tip pens; a few write in fountain pen, many write in pencil. Some writers write their first copy—their rough draft—with one kind of pencil and then switch over to something else when they begin to revise or to make changes in their writing.

°Paul Janeczko, "An Interview with Robert Cormier," *The English Journal* (September 1977).

Try experimenting with different kinds of writing implements. If you find that you are erasing a lot when you write your draft, use pencil; but also consider writing in pen and just scratching out rather than erasing. Using pen may speed up your writing process, but you may also prefer the "soft" and temporary feel that using pencil creates.

For fun, use colored markers to reflect your mood or the mood of the piece you are writing. If you are drafting an angry letter, use a red felt-tip. Use blues and greens when you are writing poems about spring or the ocean. Use red or purple for a murder mystery. Keep your journal in your favorite colors or change colors to match your mood. Write letters to family and friends in bright colors to match your stationery.

When you've finished writing your stories, poems, plays, reports, letters, journal experiments, and so forth, illustrate them with markers, crayons, and colored pencils. (We'll have more to say about preparing finished copy in Chapter 9.)

Typewriter. If you have access to a typewriter, explore how you feel using it as a tool of the trade. Some writers do all their writing, even notes and rough drafts, on typewriter. Some draft in pencil or pen and use the typewriter for final copy. Some writers like the way typing a draft gives the page the look of print; others like to shape words "by hand" with pen or pencil. You may find, too, that you prefer to do some things—like reports and stories—on the typewriter while you do others—letters, poems—by hand. In any case, typing is a good skill to learn for later in your life, so punch a few keys and see what happens.

Paper. Have on hand different kinds of paper for different kinds of writing. You can use scratch paper—inexpensive stuff, perhaps even printed already on one side—for notes and rough drafts. The back of old computer printout works well for many writers, and you can probably get piles and piles of that at school or at an office where a parent works. Some people prefer to write on lined paper, perhaps notebook pages or those long yellow "legal pads." If unlined paper is okay, you can use plain typing paper or even inexpensive mimeograph paper.

You might want to keep several colors of paper in stock. Novelist Jacqueline Susann used different colors of paper for each draft for ease in keeping track of revisions.° Save your best, most colorful paper for final drafts of papers that you want to share with others. Stationery stores and print shops have paper in many different colors and thicknesses. Paper for spirit duplicators (ditto machines) can be purchased at office supply stores in a pastel rainbow of colors. For very special copies you might want to use some rather expensive stationery or parchment paper.

Carbon paper is also a good tool of the trade to keep on hand. You can make one or more copies to share with friends, either while you are working on a piece (to get their suggestions for revision) or after you have finished (for their enjoyment). We make carbon copies of all our drafts and store them in a separate place in the house for safekeeping. More than once we've dumped a cup of coffee on a manuscript or just plain lost some pages and referred to the carbon as a backup copy.

Notebooks and Bound Books. Spiral bound notebooks come in all sizes: The smallest ones will fit in your shirt or jeans pocket, and the larger ones can fit in a portfolio and be written in on your lap. Bookstores and stationery shops also carry a variety of blank books with cloth covers. These books make especially nice journals and diaries, and they are an excellent place to make final copies of your work. In any case, as a writer you'll need one and possibly several notebooks. In Chapter Three we'll discuss using notebooks for journal-keeping, and in Chapter Four, we'll extend that to the idea of a writer's notebook. Shop around for notebooks that suit your style and personality.

Reference Books. As you write more and more, you'll probably start a collection of books that help you in your work. Some of these will be information sources, and you might want to acquire a desk encyclopedia (a one-volume storehouse of information) and even an almanac (stuffed with facts and figures about the world we live in). We keep a telephone book in our writing cranny and use it for everything from the obvious (looking up

---

°Bruce Felton and Mark Fowler, "The Writer's Life," *Writer's Digest* (January 1980).

phone numbers so we can call for information) to the less obvious (picking names at random to create characters for our short stories and novels). You'll also want to obtain some books to aid in writing correctly: a dictionary, perhaps a thesaurus (a book that gives you several words that mean the same thing), usage guide, and possibly even a typing or manuscript guide that tells you how to create professional-looking pages. We'll discuss some of these correctness guides in Chapter Nine and give you a list of titles to examine. If you really get to be an accomplished writer and start sending your work out for possible publication, you may want to buy (or ask for as a gift) a copy of *The Writer's Handbook* or *Literary Market Place*, two books that are packed with advice and hints for professional writers. Your reference collection might also include back issues of magazines for writers such as *The Writer* or *Writer's Digest*. (Check your local newsstand for this month's issue. You might enjoy getting a regular subscription.)

Getting Words on Paper

Let's say you've set aside a time to write. And you've found a comfortable place to keep your writing tools and to do the writing. And you've collected all the tools of the trade. Now what? How do you become "a writer"?

No one can give you rules to follow that will invariably work for you in getting ideas on paper. The writing process differs rather dramatically from one person to another. Some writers spend a great deal of time making notes and gathering ideas before they begin to write. Others seem to charge into a piece, writing furiously, organizing and planning as they go along. Some write nearly finished prose the first time, having thought at length about what they want to say, while others rewrite the same piece several times to get it just the way they want it. You'll have to discover what works best for you.

You'll find, too, that certain parts of the writing process are more enjoyable for you than others. Some writers love doing the research for an article or book and would be happy to spend an unlimited amount of time reading and taking notes. Others find research a necessary evil. They want their work to be credible and detailed, so they know they must do a careful job on research, but the part they like best is the actual writing. Some writers find revising the most interesting part of writing, while others are frustrated by having to change words on the page and even get angry when they didn't get their writing perfect the first time. You'll discover your own style and preference as you write more and more.

Novice writers are sometimes misled into believing that if they understand certain rules for writing, they can follow those rules in learning to write. Often the books that are used in English or language arts classes reinforce the idea of following the rules. (Years ago, those textbooks even called them the "Laws of Composition." Doesn't that sound restraining?) One textbook widely used in the schools, for example, lists patterns of development for essays: *narration, description, process, analysis, classification, comparison and contrast, definition, illustration, analogy, cause and effect*, and *argument*. The book also defines each of these. For example, it says that *analysis* "breaks a complex object or idea down into smaller, simpler elements and systematically discusses the elements in order to explain the whole." If that doesn't make sense to you, don't worry about it. We think those "patterns of development" in textbooks put the cart before the horse; they are more concerned about the *form* of writing than what goes into it: the *substance*. It may have been that sort of emphasis on form that led best-selling author Leon Uris to flunk high school English three times and reach the conclusion: "It's a good thing English and writing have nothing to do with each other."*

The point is that writers do not learn to write by learning definitions, following rules, and imitating patterns. Writers learn to write by writing. And the first requirement in getting started writing is having something to say. Before you begin writing you may not know *exactly* what you have to say about the idea in your mind, but you know that you've got an idea and

---

*Leon Uris, press release promoting *Jerusalem: Song of Songs*, published by Doubleday.

you want to write about it. You want to get it down on paper so you can think about it more clearly, appreciate it more fully, or share it with another person. At that point, you can get into a voyage of discovery, not only learning about your ideas, but discovering the process you use to get them down on paper.

Say, for example, that you and your best friend have had a fight about something you wanted to be a secret but that your friend told someone else. It's bothering you and you want to write about it, but you're not sure what the biggest issue or problem is. Are you upset that information you didn't want others to know is out? Or are you mad that your friend is not trustworthy, not someone you can count on? Or are you suspicious that your friend might be using you in some way? Does this make you worry about friendships in general? The writing process will help you clarify this.

Take another example: Last summer you had a wonderful vacation. You and your family traveled from your home to San Francisco; on the way you camped and visited Mount Rushmore, saw a rodeo in Wyoming, and hiked in Yellowstone. There were so many beautiful sights and interesting people that you would like to remember and record for the future. What should you include? What form should it take?

One more example: Your social studies teacher has assigned you a project on the Civil War. You've read the chapters in the book pretty carefully, and you even think you know that you want to do your project on the famous "march to the sea" of General Sherman. Yet, there are some gaps in your knowledge, and you don't know quite how to go about getting started writing.

In each of these cases, it might help you to begin by doing some "free writing." This simply means writing down whatever comes into your mind about a subject. You don't take a lot of time to think about what you're writing. Try to write for fifteen minutes without stopping. Don't reject any ideas; don't stop to decide what you want to throw out and what you want to keep. Author and teacher Peter Elbow says that in free writing, you can even produce "garbage," because when you finish free writing, you can throw out the garbage and keep the good stuff that's left.*

In addition, this is *not* the time to think about spelling, punctuation, or the correct choice of words. Your purpose is to discover what you think and feel, to develop the various parts of your subject, and to discover the most important elements or central points. The more you write this way the more you are likely to uncover more ideas and feelings. One session of free writing might be enough to give you ideas for your paper, but if time permits, you might do free writing on several consecutive days to figure out what you want to do with the piece. When you've finished, go through your free writing and circle all the ideas that seem especially important to you; those will be the ones you will want to focus on in your writing.

Some writers, though, don't like the idea of free writing and don't find it a useful way to get started. Some prefer to make *lists* as a way of getting started and organizing writing. You might make lists of the things your friend did that made you angry, lists of the sights on your summer vacation, lists of the key points about Sherman's march to the sea. You can make lists of things you *don't* know: what confuses you about your friend, parts of your vacation you've already forgotten, things about the Civil War that seem foggy in your brain. You can make lists of books you need to read, lists of things to do or find out before you write, lists of people you might interview before writing. The more you list on the page, the closer you are to being able to write. As you did with free writing, when you've finished your lists, circle the most important ideas. Many writers discover the form or shape of their paper just by highlighting the best ideas on their lists.

With some writing—perhaps in the case of the friend you are upset with—you may find that doing free writing to get out your feelings or just making lists is enough. Doing that will clear the air or clear your mind and clarify your feelings so you don't need to think about the problem any more. When you've finished that sort of informal writing, you may be ready to go to your friend and talk things out. Not everything you write has to take the form of a polished, finished piece to be read by other people.

On the other hand, you may have gotten a clear idea of something you

---

*Peter Elbow, *Writing without Teachers* (1974).

want to write and an audience for whom you will write it through your free writing or list making. You may have learned that you should write a letter to your friend explaining and analyzing the problem. Or you may have discovered that *you* were the problem—oversensitive, jealous—and you might enjoy writing a funny character sketch about yourself to share with the friend.

The images of your trip in the West may have triggered ideas for a series of poems. Or you might have decided to write a chronological memoir (a story told in sequence) of your trip. You may have discovered all your photographs and decided to write a set of captions for your photo album.

Free writing and list making about Sherman's march to the sea may have helped you focus your project. You've decided to make a map of the march. Or you will write a short story or imaginary diary from the point of view of a soldier on the march. Or you will do a straightforward essay or report.

Where do those ideas come from? You can't simply rely on "inspiration" in writing, but we find that if we sit at the writing desk and do some free writing and list making, pretty soon some ideas for the writing emerge. What has happened is that instead of following rules or waiting for lightning to strike, the writer has been thinking about the *substance* of the writing and how to shape ideas for an audience. Some writers call this discovering the "controlling idea" or the "lead" for a piece of writing, and once you've got it, you can plunge into the writing process.

If, after all that, you still don't have a good idea about where to go with your writing, you may want to consider "tabling" the idea, letting it simmer on the back burner of your mind for a while. Many professional writers agree that it takes a long time for an idea to ferment or percolate in their heads before they're ready to write. Don't use that as an excuse for not writing, but realize that if you can't get a handle or angle on your writing, it may simply be necessary for you to set the idea aside. You'll often discover that if you come back to it—a week later, two weeks later, six months later—what seemed a difficult writing task now looks easy.

Now you're writing your paper for real, putting your ideas down on the page. You may be writing in pencil or pen or at the typewriter. You may be writing on scruffy yellow sheets printed with dry cleaning ads on one side, or you may be putting your ideas on fancy stationery. You may be writing like mad, furiously scribbling down ideas, frustrated that you can't get your ideas down as fast as they flow from your brain. But you may be writing slowly, carefully, patiently, making certain you transfer well-formed phrases from your mind to the page just the way you want them. Once again, you'll have to discover your own style.

What you'll produce is generally called the first or "rough" draft, and it will probably need some revision and changes, a topic we'll discuss at length in Chapter Nine. Remember this, however: You'll seldom get a perfect piece of writing the first time around, and you'll need to make alterations. You may want to rewrite sections to clarify your intent or smooth out the wrinkles in your thought; you may want to make the emotions more intense in places, less so in others; you may want to tinker with your word choices, making certain you have used the most precise and vivid words to express your meaning. Good writers are good revisers.

Finally, once you've revised and rewritten, you'll want to prepare clean, final, possibly illustrated copy to share with your audience. That's the real pay off for the writing process, the time when all the hard work and hours of solitude are rewarded.

Writing with a Partner

Even though you may be very self-disciplined and have a clear sense of what you want to accomplish with your writing, you may still enjoy writing with a friend or with a small group of friends. There are several advantages to writing with a friend.

First, you can share ideas for things to write about. When you talk with other people about writing topics, they will sometimes have ideas that trigger your thinking about subjects you know well. As you sit with a friend, you can add to your lists of possible writing topics.

Second, talking about something you want to write about is an excellent way to prepare yourself to write. It works much the way free writing does: helping you sort through the good ideas and the bad, the clear and the muddy, the important and unimportant. By the time you've told your friend about your paper, you may be all but ready to write it. However, your friend can also help you at this point by asking questions about your plan. As he or she reacts, you'll learn whether your idea is clear to others, whether it needs to be expanded or contracted, even whether you need to get more information before writing your draft.

Third, writing with a partner can also help you get the actual writing done. The two of you (or a small group of friends) can set deadlines for when you will have rough drafts or sections of your writing done so you can get together and share your rough copies. If you haven't tried this, you'll be amazed at how helpful your friends can be. They can, at times, be a "make-believe" audience, reacting to your work as they think outsiders might. They can also be a real audience for your work, sharing the thrills and chills, the sobs and giggles, in what you've written.

There are dangers, of course, in working with a partner or a small group. The biggest of these, we think, is that when you and your pal(s) get together, perhaps no writing gets done. Somehow it seems easier and more fun to sit around and gab than to work on the writing. However, if you and your friend(s) are serious about writing, you'll find that you can discipline yourselves and get the work done.

Starting a Writing Club

The natural extension of writing with a partner is starting a writing club or writing group that meets regularly. We know of one group of writers in Stevens Point, Wisconsin, who have been getting together once a month since 1963. All the members of the group write and bring drafts and final copy to share at the club meetings.

Your teacher may be interested in letting you have a writing club at school, possibly meeting during school hours or just before and just after.

We've "coached" such clubs ourselves and were amazed by the number of young writers who would show up early on a cold, snowy Michigan morning to share a piece they had written.

You might, however, want to set up your club as an outside-of-school activity. Perhaps you can find or make a clubhouse in someone's cellar, barn, or attic, a place where all your members could keep writing supplies and have a special nook in which to write. The clubhouse walls could be plastered with your writing, and from time to time, the club could sponsor readings of your best and most interesting writing for parents and friends.

Consider, too, the possibility of actual publications by your club. If you have a few members and charge modest dues, you might be able to raise enough money to publish a club newsletter featuring your writing. (Sell your newsletters to friends and parents to build up the treasury; that way your newsletter can get longer and longer.)

In addition, your club might want to ask local writers—poets, novelists, writers for children, journalists—to come meet with you. These outsiders can share their own writing with you, talk about tricks of the trade, and be especially helpful to you in finding your own approach to writing.

The Writer's Journal

3

Novelist Jessamyn West has said, "I suppose journal keeping is a kind of talking to oneself."° Perhaps you have kept a diary, one with a page for each day of the week and year, and you recorded the events of the day, the experiences and feelings that had the most impact on you. Or perhaps you have a notebook that you have used on special occasions, such as when you were going through an exciting experience like a trip or when you were having a difficult time or were upset about something. For many people, writing in a journal or notebook is a way of saving and *savoring* experiences. Jessamyn West again:

> People who keep journals live life twice. Having written something down gives you the opportunity to go back to it over and over, to remember and relive the experience. Keeping a journal can also help you get perspective on your experiences. Sometimes writing something down, like talking about it, helps you understand it better.

Journals are also "comfortable" places to write because the writing is basically private, for your own enjoyment. From time to time you may want to share part of your journal with a trusted friend, but essentially you are writing for yourself. Your goal is *not* to communicate with someone else, to move or influence another person. Your aim is to capture as precisely as you can *your* perceptions, *your* emotions, *your* experiences, *your* thoughts and ideas. Your journal is a place where you can experiment with your writing and with your view of yourself, without worrying over what

° Jessamyn West, *To See the Dream* (1956, 1957).

27

other people will think. You can be wacky, sentimental, thoughtful, outrageous, comical, flamboyant, shy, or melodramatic; you can try out new opinions or new handwriting.

As a young writer, you can also use the journal as a place to save and explore writing and do your preliminary writing or drafting. You can use your journal to sharpen your writing skills as well, to practice creating detailed descriptions, to develop plot outlines for mysteries, to rehearse ideas before you put them into an essay or report.

The writer's journal or writer's notebook, then, functions not only as a way for you to capture your experiences, but as a medium through which you can develop your skills and ideas for writing. As a writer, your experiences will be an important source of material. In Chapter Four, we will suggest ways to help you develop personal experiences for writing projects. In this chapter, we will describe ways in which you can use your writer's notebook to explore your experiences, your world, and the English language.

Exploring Your Experience

Uncovering Memories. Writing about your memories gives you a chance to "live life twice." Once you start remembering, deeply buried thoughts and ideas will emerge, some that you seemingly had forgotten. Think about your past. Probe the deepest recesses of memory. What's the earliest experience you can recall? (Check the accuracy of that memory with your parents, recalling the old gag about the writer who foolishly begins his autobiography, "I remember clearly the day I was born.") Write down memories from early childhood and reflect on them, memories from your pre-school days. Recall special places and experiences from your early elementary school days. Write down some disappointments or sad times as well as good times that you can remember. Savor those experiences in your journal. *React* to them. How did those experiences help to shape you into the person you are now?

Capturing Experiences. Whether authors are writing fiction or nonfiction, poetry or drama, letters or editorials, their experiences are important, the basis for all their writing. Fiction writers and playwrights often use things that happened to them as the basis for their stories. Sometimes the things they write virtually recreate their experiences, in which case the play, story, or novel is called "autobiographical." At other times, writers use experiences as a springboard or starting point, changing ideas and characters, but using experiences in their pasts as models.

Nonfiction writers, too, draw on their experiences. A writer describing kite making or coin collecting or television writing will have some direct experience with the area he or she is writing about, having made a kite, collected some coins, or written for television. If the writer hasn't had direct experience, he or she will gain some indirectly, through reading, observing, interviewing. In both cases, those experiences can go into a journal or writer's notebook.

The experiences you save in your journal may be momentous: an automobile crash, the Indianapolis 500, meeting the President in person. But the occasion need not be something earth shattering. A birthday party, school election, haircut, or parade may provide scenes, people, emotions, physical details that you can use in your writing.

When you write about an experience, try to capture as many of its details as you can. Try to literally recreate the scene on the pages of your notebook. Describe the people, the environment, and people's reactions to the event fully. Look for details of sight, sound, even touch, taste, and smell, and put them in the journal.

After you have reported the scene or event, reflect on it. What did it mean? Why was it important? What emotions did it generate in you?

Before long, you'll have a journal chock-full of interesting word pictures and analyses of the scenes, events, and happenings in your life, and you may be surprised as you find these scenes turning up in your other writing.

Recording Dreams, Daydreams, and Nightmares. Psychologists, as well as writers and thinkers in other areas, have long held that dreams have important functions in helping people know themselves, solve problems, create ideas. Ideas and images come in dreams, ideas that seem to be unavailable to people in waking states. Some writers get ideas for whole books through their dreams, and inventors have reported coming up with some of their best ideas while asleep.

Precisely how dreams work is not clear (though it's a subject on which a number of interesting books have been written, should you be intrigued by dreams and want to know more). What's clear, however, is that while you are asleep, your subconscious mind takes over and continues to work on your experiences. Most dreams take parts of familiar experience and twist them around, put them in new situations, place them in new lights. A psychologist we know says that every dream has one foot anchored firmly in reality, while the other foot knocks down the walls and barriers of the imagination. Dreams are powerful stuff.

Many writers and psychologists suggest keeping a dream notebook. You need to keep your notebook by the side of your bed and write dreams down immediately on waking. They can slip away very quickly and huge parts may be lost before you finish breakfast. Most dream writers discover that as they maintain the notebook, they get better and better at remembering their dreams, working toward very comprehensive and detailed descriptions of their dreams. Often just describing a dream will help you understand it, but you may also enjoy playing amateur psychologist and trying to figure out *why* you dream particular things and what those dreams mean. So why were you dreaming about your worst enemy? Why did your science test loom up in a nightmare? Wasn't that dream about flying a curious one? And how about the horror of dreaming that your bicycle wouldn't move when you were fleeing a storm? You may find that as you write down and analyze your dreams, you have new ideas for stories and plays. (Many dreams can be turned into poems almost "as is.")

Another kind of dream you may write about is the daydream, or fantasy. When you fantasize, you may be anticipating likely problems (the confrontation with Dad over the lawn you forgot to mow) or unlikely problems (what it would be like if your mother died this afternoon). You may be reliving experiences as they were (the wonderful time you had at the school dance) or as you wish they had been (the fight you had with your best friend in which *you* made the crushing comeback lines). You may be thinking about a fantastic future (rock star, movie star, race car driver, basketball hero) or a realistic future (doctor, father, teacher, computer engineer). Try keeping track of some of your daydreams and fantasies in your journal. Describe them in detail. Try to interpret their meaning or figure out why they are important to you. Then think about ways you can spin your fantasies and daydreams into writing.

Analyzing Opinions. The journal is a good place to explore what you value, what you believe, what your opinions are. You can write about BIG things, like what you believe about God, war, death, or the President. You can also discover a great deal about yourself by writing about what may seem small things: why you like summer, why you find lightning scary, who your favorite teacher is, why you hate cats, what kinds of dogs you like and why, which rock group you like best, which hamburger joint makes the best french fries, which make of bicycle is best, what makes fog beautiful, why the school day should be shortened, why the administrators should let kids wear hats in school, which television programs are the best (and worst). You might like to keep lists of opinions and beliefs as they occur to you, even jotting down judgments that you make during the day. ("Wow, what an ugly hat!" "Not me! I'd never do a thing like that!" "That's unfair!") Transfer those to your journal and write about them when you get home.

As you analyze a belief, try tracing its history in your mind. Is this something your parents believe or taught you to believe? Did you once have an experience that shaped your opinion or reaction? Have a series of experiences influenced you? Is this something you have always believed? Do your friends believe it? Do your teachers? Is this something you've changed your mind about recently? Knowing the source of something you believe makes the difference between having a belief and having a prejudice.

Developing Use of Your Senses. Writers rely on their senses—sight, touch, hearing, smell, taste—to describe the world so their readers can experience their vision. As a writer you will need to sharpen your sensory awareness. J. W. Patrick Creber, a British teacher and poet, says, "Much adolescent inarticulateness has its roots in a blunted sensibility."° What he says about adolescents goes for adults, too: Because we fail to use our senses fully to absorb our world, we sometimes write about it inarticulately. Powerful language, in short, grows from powerful use of the senses to see and experience the world.

Use your notebook to collect sensory experiences. Sit in one place—your backyard, a park, the library, a fast food restaurant—for thirty minutes with your notebook in hand and write down everything you:

—Hear. Listen for sounds in the distance or background sounds as well as sounds right near you; listen to people sounds, machine sounds, nature sounds.

—Smell. This one is harder; one smell may predominate, but try to detect changes, differences, mixes.

—Taste. Harder still, unless you're eating something while you write.

—Feel. Notice the texture of your clothes, the pressures against you; feel your chair, table, notebook, paper; tune into the feeling of the air, the sun on your skin.

—See. This is the easiest and you could write forever on what you see, but look for subtleties and nuances—shade, shadows, changes in light, bright spots, dirt, cobwebs in the corner—as well as the big and obvious things.

On another occasion, take time to focus on one sense and develop your awareness of that sense and describe that sense in detail. Take fifteen minutes to describe everything you hear, for example. You may be surprised at how much information a single sense can give you.

Also try describing all the senses involved in a single activity. When you eat a hamburger, for example, what do you see, hear, feel, taste, and smell?

°J. W. Patrick Creber, *Sense and Sensitivity* (1965).

What senses are involved when you take a shower? What do your senses tell you when you are sitting in the middle of social studies class?

You may find describing sensations difficult. Try using comparisons to get at the precise feeling you are trying to capture. Perhaps the upholstery of the chair feels like caterpillar skin, or the blue-white haze over the sun looks like your living room drapery liners, or your sticky summer skin makes you feel as if you've been working all day at the cotton candy booth at the fair. (When writers make comparisons like these, they're making *metaphors*, and metaphoric writing is very common in fiction, poetry, and even in nonfiction.)

Exploring Your World

Exploring your world in your journal is a natural extension of sharpening responses to your own experience. Now's the time to move out beyond your day-to-day events and happenings to seek out new ideas. Try some of the following in your journal.

Recording New Impressions. When you first meet someone, take a little time afterward to write about that person. Describe the physical appearance, the mannerisms, your impressions about the person's character and personality, your guesses about his/her values and ideas, your sense of his/her language and ways of expressing ideas. (At a later date, go back and review those impressions. Were you right?) Describe first impressions of a new teacher, a new place like a park or building or game room or food store, a new game or toy, a new television program, a new pet. Trace your new experiences in writing.

Analyzing Experience. A writer is not only interested in what happens, but *why* it happens. That's called *analysis*. Try to figure out why and how things work (or don't work). Fill journal pages with your analyses of the world. You can analyze:

—Events. How did that fire start? Why did we lose the game? How did that person get elected? What caused the accident? How did I fail that test?

—People. Why is Mr. Green so crabby? What makes Eric such a good football player? What makes Joanie so much fun? Why is Michael so sad?

—Groups. What are some common traits of musicians? of teachers? of athletes? of the "smart" kids? (Avoid stereotypes as you make these generalizations, but try to discover common qualities that are *real* and observable for the group.)

—Movies and television. What is the "formula" for television situation comedies? for soap operas? for outer space movies? for Burt Reynolds movies? for *Sesame Street*? (A good test of the accuracy of your analysis is to see if you can write a page or two of sample script in imitation of the program or film.)

—Ideas and concepts. What is love? friendship? honesty? fear? Look beyond stereotypes or "stock" descriptions of these abstractions to find out what they really mean. What does the idea that "all people are created equal" mean to you? Do you believe that "anything worth having is worth fighting for"? Listen for other ideas in school and at home and describe what they mean to you.

Evaluating Experience. Every day of our lives we make judgments about people, places, events. "That was a great movie." "He's a marvelous cook." "What a dumb idea!" You will also make judgments of many different kinds as you write, and it's important to make good solid evaluations, not just to flip off unsubstantiated opinions. Use your journal to explore your values and the world around you. Write short film reviews (not just whether the movie was good or bad, but what was good or bad about it), book reviews (of your free reading or required reading for school), events around your school, community, church, home. Always, as you write, try to focus on why you believe what you believe, on the *criteria* or *values* you are using to make judgments.

Exploring Your World Through the Newspaper. As you extend your experience and write about the world, pretty soon you'll want to think and write about events that are "outside of walking distance," events that you cannot experience firsthand. Nevertheless, you can still examine these through your writing journal, and the newspaper makes an excellent source of ideas and materials. Set aside some time each day to study the newspaper. If you read the paper after others have finished with it, you may want to clip stories and articles that you find especially intriguing or thought provoking. Then write reactions and responses in your journal. Among the kinds of articles you might clip and write about are:

—News stories telling about local, regional, state, national, and world events.

—Editorials and commentaries evaluating problems in our society and making recommendations.

—Feature articles on business, contemporary living, the arts, books, films.

—Sports stories and articles.

If you analyze the paper regularly, you may soon find yourself ready to write a letter to the editor expressing your opinion, an activity we take up in more detail in Chapter Five.

Exploring Language

Most writers are intrigued by language—words, sentences, stories, turns-of-phrase—and take pleasure from studying how the English language (or any other language) operates. You can use your journal to heighten your awareness of language and simply to store unusual or interesting expressions that you run across or create.

Collecting Dialogues and Dialects. When you write drama and fiction (and even some kinds of nonfiction), the way people talk will be important. Spend time listening to the language of people around you, attending to both *what* they say and *how* they say it. To develop your ear for how people's language reflects their personalities, listen carefully to conversations. Observe whether people put their ideas in the form of statements, questions, or demands. Do they come right to the point when they talk, or do they beat around the bush? Do they use formal words or informal words? How does one person's language differ from someone else's? For practice, write down short conversations you hear, trying to capture the essence of a person's language in writing.

Listen for traces of *dialect* in conversation. Dialects are simply regional variations of language, and a dialect will often tell you something about where a person came from. You can't, in writing, represent all features of a dialect, such as those that involve tone of voice or the speed with which a person talks. But you can represent and study:

—Word choices. Listen to different words people use for the same things. Do they say "pop" or "soda" or "tonic" to describe a soft drink? Do they say "dinner" or "supper"? "telephoned" or "called"? "stockings" or "nylons"? "sneakers" or "tennies" or "gym shoes"? "parlor" or "living room"? "refrigerator" or "icebox"? Sometimes word choices differ from one generation to another (older people are more likely to say "parlor" than others), but often these word choices grow from regional dialects ("tonic" is a uniquely New England expression, for example).

—Grammatical usage. What different forms of usage do you hear spoken? Some people say: "I don't want no juice." Others: "I don't want any juice." Some: "I ain't seen him." Others: "I haven't seen him." You've probably studied these usage patterns in school and may have been taught that some are "wrong" or "bad English." Although some usage items are not considered acceptable in formal speech and writing, most usage items are "right" in the sense that they communicate a message effectively. For the writer, they are a marvelous resource, because you can often make your characters in fiction come alive by having them speak in dialect, and you can even use dialect in nonfiction writing to capture the essence of a person you are describing.

—Pronunciations and curiosities. Practice trying to capture the way a person talks in dialect, especially a person whose pronunciation is different from your own. (Writing this way is called "eye dialect," meaning that a reader can study it and get a sense of how a character talks.)

You might practice, for example, writing dialect of a speaker from New England:

"I pahked the cah in the lawt while we went to the wawf [wharf] fuh lobstuhs."

Or from the Deep South:

"Unhayund me, suh. No genlmun would behayve as y'all are."

Or from the Far West:

"Hold on, there, pardner. Ah may jest shoot!"

Of course, what we've written here are stereotypes of those dialects. Listen for them yourself in *real* conversation and write some eye dialect of your own. Then use that skill in your writing.

Collecting Words and Expressions. In your reading or television or movie watching or in listening to people talk, you will come across new and interesting uses of words. Write them down and keep track of the situation or circumstances in which you heard them. At first you may just guess at some meanings. The dictionary may help with the meaning, but seeing or hearing the word in context will give you a much clearer idea of what the speaker or author is trying to say.

Collect images and metaphors that you especially like. Perhaps they paint a picture that you can really see, or they capture an emotion that helps you understand what the speaker or author is trying to say.

Collect puns and plays on words that are clever and amusing. We have recently enjoyed collecting the names of businesses that use word play in their titles: "The Puppet Tree" (["puppetry"] for a puppet store), "Just Desserts" (a snack shop), "The Growing Concern" (a nursery), and "Tread Quarters" (a tire store).

Riddles are also often based on puns or plays on words.
For example:

QUESTION: What's black and white and red/read all over?
ANSWER: A newspaper or an embarrassed zebra.

Advertisements often use puns or plays on words to attract your attention.

A bookstore in our neighborhood prides itself on having recent releases as soon as they're out. It's called the Community News Center and boasts that "News is our middle name."

You can also use your journal to create words and expressions, to play with language. Make up words that do what you want them to. A good word for those spring afternoons in school when you can't seem to stay awake and listen to what the teacher says might be a "snoozler." You might call the person who can't make the big play in a big game the "chokester." You might explain to your parents why your room is a disaster area by telling them it was "bomboozled."

Create new metaphors to replace the old, worn clichés. How else can you describe beauty than by saying, "She was pretty as a picture?" Think of comparisons you can make to replace "good as gold," "clear as a bell," "sharp as a tack." Think of new ways to "bite the bullet" or to become "sadder but wiser." Think of something that is even less than "the tip of the iceberg" or someone who grew by other than "leaps and bounds."

Create your own puns. Look for and listen to words that have double meanings, that can be used in more than one way. Perhaps you have heard this exchange:

HE: "Well . . ."
SHE: "That's a deep subject."

Think about words that have the same sound but different meanings (homonyms) and the possibilities they allow for word play: *knight* and *night*, *dear* and *deer*. Play with words that have multiple meanings such as *run*, *dumb*, or *suit*.

Copying Quotes. Often in your reading you will find passages or lines that impress you. Copy them in your journal where you can go back and reread them from time to time. The things that you respond to also create a record of your growth and thinking and give you insight into what you appreciate in writing. Some writing teachers even think that copying in modest quantities helps a writer improve his or her style, by helping the writer *feel* how other writers have done things with language.

The Journal Habit

For some people, notebooks and journals become an integral part of their lives, and they always have a volume close at hand for capturing a moment, for saving ideas for future projects, for keeping track of what's happening to them, for clarifying their thoughts and making them conscious of their feelings. After years of journal keeping, they have a library shelf filled with volumes of their own writing, a real treasure for themselves and for their children and relatives.

To make your journal a rewarding, habit-forming experience, there are a few things to keep in mind. First of all, your journal is a place for you to explore and experiment, and thus it is a private book of writing. When you are writing for yourself, don't take time to worry about perfect spelling and punctuation. Sometimes when you concentrate on those things, you lose track of ideas you are attempting to get down on the page.

Related to that, you have a right to be *tentative* in your journal, expressing doubts and uncertainties, writing down half-crazy ideas that you're not certain about. If you haven't worked something out just right in your mind, don't worry about it. Put it in your journal and come back to work on the fine details of the idea later.

Don't wait to write things down. Though you may have a set time to work on your journal, carry a scratch pad or note cards with you to write things down as they happen. And write things down in full and glorious detail. Sometimes if you "censor" yourself too much or worry about revising or refining what you write in your journal, you will end up by losing an idea, discarding it before you've really had a chance to test it to see if it would take you anywhere.

And finally, don't throw anything away. Sometimes you will write something and look back at it a few days later and think it was silly or immature or just plain dumb. However, keep in mind that one of the things you want from your journal is a record of your growth as a person and as a writer.

What Shall I Write About?

4

The question that titles this chapter is one of the most perplexing, difficult, and downright maddening ones writers must ask themselves. At the same time, it is one of the easiest and simplest to answer.

How can it be both?

The difficult part is that when ideas leave you, or when you lose confidence that your ideas will be interesting to another person, you feel absolutely empty—lost, with no place to go. Where can one go to get that all-important good idea? Jonathan Swift, the British poet and satirist wrote:

Be mindful when invention fails,
to scratch your head, and bite your nails.°

You can do more than scratch your head and bite your nails, however. Here is the simple solution to writer's block that we mentioned:

Write from your own experience.

Yet even as you read that solution, we suspect you recognized:

That's not so simple.

Your experience is incredibly, astonishingly, extraordinarily complex. Literally from the moment you were born you have been soaking up impressions from the world around you. As a baby you were bombarded by

---

°Jonathan Swift, "On Poetry" (1733).

40

sounds and bright lights at the moment of birth that probably frightened you. Gradually, though, you were able to recognize sights and sounds and tastes and smells. At two months of age—more or less—you smiled at friendly faces. By six months, you knew that a particular kind of jar contained your favorite baby food, and you would growl and smile when you saw it. By then, too, you knew that if you squalled loud enough, someone would show up and give you something to eat or change your uncomfortable diaper or hold you for a while.

By the time you were eighteen months old, you had begun to develop a very useful tool to help you sort through and organize your experiences: language. You had already learned a few words—*dog, ball, milk, Mama*—that you used to identify familiar objects. Now you started to string those words together into short sentences—"Allgone milk." "Byebye Mama"—to describe what you were thinking and feeling.

In the years since then, millions of sense impressions have entered your mind every day, and you've spent much of your life—waking and even asleep—trying to interpret those impressions, using language to help in the process. You use words to categorize and file experiences under similar headings. You also use language to call up your experiences from memory and to organize them for other people:

"Let me tell you what I did in school today."

"Hey, did you hear about Sam's bicycle?"

"What happens if you mix vinegar and baking soda?"

Spoken language, whether conversation, gossip, or discussion, is one way people exchange ideas and experiences. Writing is another, and writing is one of the most useful ways for one person to share experiences with another.

So don't ever say, "I haven't got anything to write about." Your head is jam-packed with ideas to share. And don't ever say, "Nobody would ever want to read about *my* experiences." From the beginning of written history, writers have agreed on the rule-of-thumb for this chapter:

Write from your own experience.

Of course, that "rule" is also a *cliché* or *bromide*, a word or expression used so often it becomes commonplace. William Lynott, a freelance writer, explains:

> If you want to see a youngster wince, just say, "Brush after every meal."
>
> The problem with bromides like that is that we hear them too often. . . . "Eat your vegetables; they're good for you!"
>
> For writers, it's "Write about what you know!"°

Even though it's a cliché, Lynott explains, it is one that he has to relearn from time to time. Every once in a while, he observes, he sails off into the blue, writing about things outside his experience. But the writing seems flat and hollow. The writing he gets published comes from what he knows.

He adds, however, that writing about what you know and what you have experienced doesn't mean that you actually have to *do* everything before you write about it. You don't have to die to write a good death scene. You don't have to have been lost in an airplane to write a spine-chilling story about the Bermuda Triangle. Your imagination can help you take your past experiences and project them into unfamiliar or new situations. Ned Roren says, "A writer needn't go out and live, but stay home and invent."† We don't agree that one shouldn't or needn't "go out and live." A writer should be an active liver-of-life, collecting as many diverse experiences as possible. Roren's point, however, is that you can also live and write from your own experience just by sitting at your writing desk and turning your imagination loose.

Jules Verne, the author of *Twenty Thousand Leagues Under the Sea*, could create his futuristic vision of a submarine by thinking about his knowledge of the sea and his knowledge of scientific principles, then letting his imagination go to work, projecting those ideas into a new situation. As a writer, you can compose essays and poems and stories about the past, the

---

°William J. Lynott, "I Know, I Know," *Writer's Digest* (December 1982).
†Barbara Rowes, *The Book of Quotes* (1979).

future, and things fantastic, but you still need to root that writing in your present experience and knowledge.

You can't write from your own experience if you don't pay close attention and think about the life you are leading. The novelist Ernest Hemingway once remarked:

> The worst poverty anyone can have is a poverty of mental interests. Money does not remove it and it does you no good to travel because you take it with you wherever you go.*

Writers tend to be curious, interested people who like to think about their lives and experiences, whose minds constantly percolate with ideas, topics, and questions.

We suspect that because you are interested in writing you do *not* have the "poverty of mental interests" described by Hemingway, that you have a mind chock-full of ideas to write about. As a writer, you'll find it helpful to make some lists of your possibilities so you can think about what you know, what you have done in your time on this planet, and how that can be turned into writing.

Inventorying Your Experience

In the last chapter we introduced you to the writing journal and suggested that you keep a journal as a running record of reactions to experience. Now we'll suggest that you set aside a few pages of that journal to make an *inventory* of your experience—a listing of what you've done, what you've seen, what you think is important, what you want to have happen to yourself and to the world. Use the questions and topics that follow to jog your memory. You can write this inventory all at once, taking an hour or two to complete it, or you might want to use the ideas in this chapter over a period of several months, coming back to your journal from time to time to enter more writing ideas.

---

*Ernest Hemingway, letter to Carol Hemingway, from *Ernest Hemingway: Selected Letters*, Carlos Baker, ed. (1981).

This we guarantee: If you'll take time to conduct a careful inventory, you'll create a storehouse of writing ideas that can last for years. We can't guarantee that you'll never have writer's block again—that you'll never "scratch your head and bite your nails"—but we're confident that you will have a rich resource to which you can turn.

(Note: Use a fresh page of your journal for each of the categories that follow.)

Areas of Expertise

What do you know a great deal about? What are your hobbies? some areas where you spend a considerable amount of time reading? Jot these in your journal, since each is an "area of expertise," an area with which you already have experience and knowledge. What do you know more about than most people your age? How did you get this special knowledge? Why is it interesting and important to you? (Put these ideas in your journal.) What are your outside-of-school interests? What do you do to earn money in your spare time or to fill up empty summer hours? What can you fix or repair or put together? What arts and crafts can you do? List all these areas of expertise and use them as starting points for writing.

Firsts and Landmarks

Write down some of the "firsts" in your life. Can you remember your first day at school? What was that like? What is the first memory you have of *any*thing? What was your first pet? If you've ever fallen in love (or "in like"), list your first love (or first "like"). List your:
—first trip to the dentist.
—first taste of pizza (or any other food you especially like).
—first time in church or synagogue.
Think about firsts that were sad or unfortunate for you. Can you recall having a person close to you become very ill or even die? Put that down as something you might write about. Can you remember putting the first scratch on a new bike or breaking a new toy? Think of as many other firsts as you can and list them in your journal.

Lasts

We'll leave it to you to think of some "lasts" in your life.

People

Draw a small circle on a clean page of your journal and put an X in the center to represent yourself. Then, in ever-widening circles, list the people who are special or important to you. Start by surrounding the X with the names of people who are especially close to you: your family, your relatives, your very best friends. Draw another circle to enclose them. Next move outward and list other people: people you know and like around town, people who have influenced your life in important ways. Draw a third circle around them. Now think about people who are even further away, perhaps even people you haven't met: movie stars, rock stars, sports idols, political figures. Draw a circle to include them. Then change gears by listing *imaginary* people, folks who are figments of your imagination: characters in a story or play you might like to write, a person your age who has all the traits you'd like to see in yourself, fantasy creatures, outer space beings. (Remember what William Lynott and Ned Roren said: that you don't have to have had actual experience with people to write about them.) Finally, around the edge of your paper list any people we've forgotten to mention but who are interesting or important to you. (A sample of how your diagram might look is shown in Figure 2.)

Places

On another journal page, list places, starting with every interesting place you've visited in your life. These don't have to be just places where you've gone on vacation; they can be places like zoos or museums you've visited on school field trips. They can be special places or "hangouts" where you spend a lot of time. Then list places you've heard about and think you might like to visit (not limiting yourself to this planet). As you did for the "People" category, list some *imaginary* places: the site of a fantasy story you'd like to write, the setting for a crime story, a new planet that is undiscovered in our solar system, a place where you'd like to live someday.

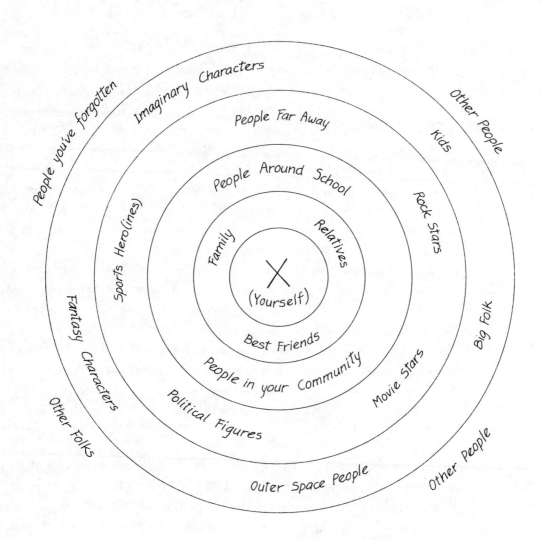

Figure 2

Memories

Write down memories of the best times in your life: moments of triumph. Times when you did especially well at something. Moments that you'd like to go back and relive sometime. Now list the not-so-good times in your life. Even though such experiences were not very pleasant for you, it is often useful for you to go back to recapture those moments in writing. What would you do differently this time? How would you change the "story" of that bad time if you could?

Books

Write down titles of some of the books you've read that you have most enjoyed. Then, when you are looking for something to write about, spend time recalling—in writing—your favorite book. Why was it special for you? Write down the names of some of the characters from your favorite books and consider writing original stories about them. List your favorite authors. Why do you enjoy their books? You might write a fan letter to one of those authors or write a story in imitation of his or her style.

Media: TV, Radio, Records, Film

List your favorites in these categories. Then write down your *un*-favorites: the TV programs, radio shows, records, and movies that you despise. You can write about either kind—the goodies or the baddies—or you can write about the differences between the good and the bad. What makes a film good? What does a record have to do to make it onto *your* hit parade? Also jot down ideas for television programs you'd like to see on the air. (You can probably write a letter to a station manager or network president with your suggestion. Or you can write a sample script for the show.) Put down your ideas for smash hit films. What kind of movie would appeal to the kids you know? Think about books that would make best-sellers among your friends. Later you might even take a crack at writing one of those books.

Things to Change

Nobody's life is perfect, and there are probably a lot of things in your life that you'd like to change. Start by writing down some things you'd like to see changed around home. (It's okay to be critical about things around home, especially when you're writing in your private journal or diary. Sometime you can do writing that will help you think about changing some of the things you don't especially like, possibly sharing that writing with family members.) List things to change around school: homework (of course), what you're learning, discipline codes, even the bell schedule (does school start too early for you?). Next describe things to change around town. Are there problems your community needs to solve? Think about this nation and even the whole world; don't be bashful about writing down your ideas for a better planet. What, in your view, needs to be altered in the world in which we live?

Questions

We're going to guess that as a person interested in writing, you constantly bubble with questions. A lot of people become writers, not because they have lots to say right now, but because they have intellectual curiosity, and that curiosity leads them to inquire about all manner of things. Here are some questions people have raised from time to time. Read them, then make a list of the questions you think are important:

—What makes the universe run?

—What are objects made of?

—What is God like?

—Is there life after death?

—Why do bad things happen?

—Is it better to be rich than happy? (Can one be both?)

—Did Benjamin Franklin really invent all those things?

Questions. Questions. Questions.

The list can go on and on.

It *should* go on and on, and you may want to leave a few extra pages in your journal so you can add more questions to your list.

Everything Else
(or Miscellaneous)

What have we left out? You can see pretty clearly what we mean when we say you can write from your own experience. There's more inside you yet: ideas and memories that don't fit our categories. Take some time, then, and rack your brain for other thoughts and opinions. Get them listed in your journal so you can begin drawing on them as you write in the future.

Developing Writing Ideas

Okay. So you've got a journal and you've started listing ideas so you can write from your experience. How do you go about turning those ideas into writing?

The answer to that question may seem obvious to you, and as you jotted down ideas about people, places, questions, and so on, you may have felt ready to write, itching to get out a stack of blank paper and to begin pouring out your story. If that's the case, we say, "Bravo! Go to it." Spend the rest of the afternoon or morning or evening doing what this book is about: writing.

Sometimes, though, even when you seem to have a good idea, you don't know quite how to go about transferring it to paper. The actual shape of the writing isn't clear to you, or you don't quite know how to begin it or how to approach it. This section is designed to help you develop some of those writing ideas further, so as you begin writing, you'll have a clear idea of what you want to do and a plan of action.

Thinking About Audience and Purpose

We'll take a couple of hypothetical or imaginary writing ideas and discuss some ways of developing them. Let's say one of your writing ideas listed in the inventory is to describe someone you met recently, perhaps an interesting musician or a crafts person or a long-lost cousin. We'll call this the "Person Paper." For the other illustration, we'll take that inventory category of "Things to Change" and we'll suppose you want to accomplish something around school: getting the principal to establish a new literary magazine for blossoming writers like yourself.

You've got the basic topics for both papers. How do you develop them?

A good first step is to describe—either in your head or on a page of your journal—the *audience* for the paper. There are times, of course, when you'll be writing something for your eyes only, in which case you can skip this step. For most writing, however, you'll want a readership. Why go to all the trouble of writing and then not have any readers?

To discover an audience, flip back in your journal to the inventory section labeled "People." Look at the circle chart you created there describing people: close to you, around school and town, far away, and so on. That sketch of people can provide you with ideas for audiences for your writing.

Who would want to read the "Person Paper"? Certainly your close friends will want to read about this interesting character. So will your parents. If you're writing about a relative, that person and his or her family would probably like to see a copy. If you're writing about a craftsperson, that person and his/her associates would like to read it, and they might even want to run off copies to use in publicizing their work.

Would your favorite rock star be interested in the "Person Paper"? Probably not, unless it's about him or her. Would the mayor of your town? Only if it is well written and about a person of some local prominence (or about the mayor him- or herself).

The "Change Paper" would have a different audience. Again, your parents and friends would probably enjoy reading your proposal for change, but the real audience is the person in power: the principal. You'll probably want to write this paper as a letter or proposal addressed directly to him or her. What about reaching other readers, though? You might write one version of your letter for the school newspaper, or the editor might invite you to do an article about your proposal. Certainly your teacher and classmates would be a good audience, and they could even give you helpful advice following some of your rough drafts.

You can see, then, that the audience will differ for almost everything you write.

To help you further clarify your knowledge and plans for the audience, use your journal to write a short "character sketch" of your proposed readers. What are they like? What do they like to read? What will your writing have to do to attract and retain their attention?

Describing your audience will lead you directly into describing the *purpose* or *aim* of your piece. What do you want to accomplish with this writing? What do you want to have it do for and to your readers?

For the "Person Paper" your aim may simply be to inform or entertain. That's an excellent reason for writing: You met a unique person, and now you want to share your enjoyment with others. For the "Change Paper" your purpose is more serious, for you intend to get the principal to act on what you propose.

Again using your journal, write a short statement of purpose, for example:

"I want to describe my cousin Phil so clearly that people can understand what a wacky, funny, but caring person he is."

"I want to write a letter to the principal that is so persuasive he'll let us start the new literary magazine right away."

When you've finished drafting your paper, look back over this statement of purpose. Does your writing seem aimed toward it? (You may also discover through writing that you didn't have your purpose clearly in mind; if so, that would be a good time to rewrite the statement.)

Choosing a Form of Writing

Thus far we've used the term "paper" to describe writing in this chapter. In real life, however, people don't just write "papers"; they write *poems* or *plays* or *essays* or *stories* or *postcards* or *scripts* or *memoirs*. These are called forms or modes of discourse. To get focus into your writing plans, always think about the form of discourse you want to use. You may be surprised at the number of possibilities that exist. For example, with your "Person Paper," you might think that the only thing to do is to tell a story about the person. But consider some of the following possibilities.

—You could write a *character sketch* of the person, drawing (in words) what he or she is like.

—You could write a *reminiscence* or *memoir* telling of your times with the person.

—You could write a *dialog* between yourself and the person, a real conversation written down, or one you make up that catches the spirit of the person.

—You could write a *play* featuring that person.

For your "Change Paper" consider some of the following possibilities:

—a *letter* to the principal asking for his or her attention to your request.

—an *editorial* for your school paper.

—a *letter to the editor* of the school paper.

—an *oral presentation* to the principal, in which you read your proposal face-to-face.

—a *slide tape* or *videotape* arguing your case, perhaps with you and some other students reading your creative writing aloud to demonstrate the need for a new magazine.

—a *bulletin board display* of writing, along with an appeal for support for the literary magazine.

To help you think of some possibilities, we've listed some discourse forms and modes in Figure 3. Whenever you start to write (or at least until ideas pop into your mind spontaneously), consult the list and explore new possibilities. You can also add to the list as you see new and interesting forms in books, newspapers, and magazines.

How do you create these different forms of writing? If you've never written a play or poem or letter to the editor, you may not feel you know enough to begin. Here is some help from British writer Ben Jonson, who said hundreds of years ago:

For a man to write well, there are required three necessaries—to read the best authors, observe the best speakers, and much exercise of his own style.*

(We assume that Ben Jonson meant men *and* women writers in this statement.) What he's saying is that to learn different styles or modes of discourse you should:

1. Read a lot.
2. Listen a lot.
3. Practice, practice, practice.

If you are going to write a letter to the editor, for example, get a copy of a newspaper and read the Letters page. Which letters seem effective to you? Which ones miss the mark? What's the difference in content and style? Soon you'll find yourself developing criteria to evaluate letters to the editor; you'll have taught yourself the style.

If you are writing a play, see some plays presented on stage, even plays by an amateur theater group. If you can't see live plays, pretend your television set is a playhouse and evaluate what you see. What makes an interesting, lively play? What makes a snoozer? Study how characters make entrances and exits, how they talk to one another, how the playwright heightens suspense. Then go to the library and check out a book of plays. Study how they are presented in print. After you've read and observed and evaluated, head off and write your play.

In short, we're suggesting that as a writer, you should be a careful observer of speech and writing in the world around you. (See also Chapter Three, where we suggested that you write in your journal about interesting uses of language you observe.) You should constantly be aware of how other writers are using language and how you can draw on their experience in your own work.

---

*Ben Jonson, *Timber; or, Discoveries* (1640).

Figure 3 *Some Forms of Writing*

Many of these forms will be discussed in more detail in the next several chapters. If you don't recognize a form or know what it is, don't worry. Just read on.

Journals and diaries (you already know about these, but consider imaginary journals and diaries of characters you invent)

Sense impressions (writing down things as they flow through your mind and senses)

Anecdotes (stories from your experience)

Sketches (pictures in words of people, places, events)

On-the-Scene Reports (newspaper style, of happenings around your home, school, or city)

Autobiography (a chapter or two about your life)

Biography (the story of someone else's life, someone you know or someone you've read about)

Monologue (a "conversation with yourself" either written down or tape recorded)

Dialog (a conversation with two people, real or imaginary)

Short Story (adventure, science fiction, western, historical, romance)

Novel (a full-length work of fiction, perhaps done in collaboration with a friend)

Riddles, Puzzles, and Jokes

"Framing" or Planning Your Paper

There are many different ways to get organized for writing, once you've settled on your purpose, audience, and the form of writing. Some teachers will tell you always to present your ideas in a formal outline like the following:

Poetry (rhymed or unrhymed, haiku, cinquain, sonnets, couplets, greeting card verses)

Songs (lyrics for old songs or lyrics for songs you write)

Letters (to friends, enemies, parents, relatives, editors, public figures, imaginary beings)

Telegrams (real or imaginary)

Reviews (of books, movies, films)

Newspaper and Magazine Articles (informing and entertaining)

Cartoon Strips (with your own or a partner's drawings)

How-to Books (describing what you can do well)

Directions (for making things, going places)

Advertisements (real or made up, promoting ideas and events)

Commercials (for television and radio)

Fact Books (strange but true)

Record Books (school sports and academic achievements)

Posters (to display in your room, to advertise something)

Satire (making fun of things through writing)

Plays (puppet plays, one-acts, skits, television or radio)

Slide Tapes (colored slides to accompany a script)

Bulletin Boards (a display of your and others' writing)

Neighborhood Newspaper (print it yourself)

Prophesies and Predictions (guesses about the future)

Science Reports (about the natural world)

Math Problems and Stories (invent your own math exercises)

I. Main Point
   A. part of the main point
      1. part of the part of the main point
         a. part of the part of the part, etc.

That style of planning works for some school reports (a topic we'll explore in Chapter Seven). For your out-of-school writing, something a little less formal will do nicely.

In fact, some writers don't even use a written plan at all; once they have their writing idea in mind, they simply begin at the beginning and write their way to the end. (Novelists regularly say they don't know how their stories will end until they actually write them.) Planning in your head or planning as you go along will work for you if you're very confident and clear about what you are going to say. Most writers, though, prefer to have some sort of written plan.

We prefer something in between the formal outline and not writing down anything at all. We call it "framing" a paper. Just as a carpenter puts up a "frame" or a skeleton of a house before tacking on the outside walls, a writer needs to build a frame for a paper. We also like the term "frame" because it reminds us of a picture frame: What you're doing when you frame a piece of writing is planning and writing down a "picture" you plan to create and frame for your audience.

We begin framing by making lists of the things we want to include in a piece of writing, then start adding and subtracting ideas. The page that we used in framing this chapter is shown in Figure 4, so you can see its informality. That "frame" is cleaner than some we do. Often by the time we've written a chapter, the planning sheet is so covered with notes and scratchings that it's almost indecipherable.

Some writers use scraps of paper or notecards to frame their writing, spreading the cards out on a table or desk and then pushing them around until a good organization appears. Others insist on doing a neatly typed "abstract" (a summary-in-advance). Many writers nowadays use a tape recorder to do their planning, talking to the machine and transcribing later. We've even planned book chapters on paper napkins at McDonald's.

Whatever method of planning you choose, it is important that you do plan, that you think about what you're going to write before you actually write. We think you'll save yourself a lot of revising if you plan carefully before writing.

Four: WHAT SHALL I WRITE ABOUT?

Beginning: Question of this chapter a difficult one, and simple.   *[Jonathan Swift quote Tyrott]*
    Simple--write from experience, quotes from writers on that
    Not-so-simple--experience is complex
    How we use language from childhood to shape experience

Experience Inventory (explain):
    Areas of Expertise
    Firsts and Landmarks
    People
    Places
    Memories (Fond/Not-So-Fond) *[2 categories?]*
    Books
    Media (TV/Film etc.)   *[Add Ned Rosen quote]*
    Things to Change
    ~~Visions of the Future~~   *[Covered in Chapter three]*
    Questions
    Misc.   *~~Street Notebook~~ or Writer's Notebook*

Developing writing ideas. So you've got a notebook and etc. chock
full. How do you go about getting them down.   *[Hemingway on Poverty of Experience]*

Step 1. Audience and purpose.

Step 2. Discourse Forms and Modes
        Personal Writing
        Creative Writing
[Don't do these as steps]   Public/Persuasive--------Do outside reading and looking
        Oral and Drama   about. Jonson Quote
        Media Forms
               [Do on insert page]

~~Step 3.~~ Plan or outline

        Formal outline (OK for some situations)   *[Use the "Framing" metaphor here]*
        Informal outlines
        Conversation with friend, imagined
         New Heading : The Act of Writing
~~Step 4.~~ Write--writing blocks
      Freewriting
      Start with Paragraph 2
      Write the ending

      Quotes on seat-of-the-pants writing   *[~~Wersba~~ Maybe Nathaniel Benchley]*

Jesse Stuart: Write to Please Yourself

Figure 4

The Act of Writing

Let's review where we've been in this chapter.

We first suggested that you write from your own experience and had you jot down ideas in an experience inventory.

Then we said it's a good idea to think about the audience for your writing and your purpose in writing.

Next we suggested that you think about a form of discourse for your piece.

Finally, we argued that you need to "frame" your paper before you write.

All that may seem rather complex and complicated, but once you've written a few times, you'll see that the various tasks flow into one another pretty smoothly. If you're not at this stage already, you'll soon discover that paper ideas often come "allatonce," so you suddenly "know" about purpose, audience, discourse form, and frame in a rush as an idea comes to you.

In any case, it's now time to write.

For many writers, the real moment of truth comes when they sit down and begin making marks on the page—drafting. Even though a writer has prepared carefully, sometimes all ideas fly out the window and the writer is back at the beginning: "I haven't got anything to say." This is another form of writer's block. We hope it doesn't happen to you, but if it does, there are several strategies you can try.

First, it's important for you to know there's no such thing as "inspiration" in writing, a magic flash of lightning that will get you going. Barbara Wersba, a writer for young adults, says:

> If you wait for inspiration at your desk, you will wait the rest of your life. . . .
> The whole secret of writing is to go to the desk every day of your life and
> put in a certain number of hours.°

°Paul Janeczko, "An Interview with Barbara Wersba," *The English Journal* (November 1976).

Now, you're not a professional writer, so it's not necessary for you to write *every* day. However, Wersba's point is valid for all writers: Sitting at the desk is the key. When it's time to write, *sit down and do it*. We've found dozens and dozens of times in our own work that if we simply go to the study and start writing, pretty soon the ideas start to flow and we get something down on paper. It may not be the best stuff we've ever written, but it gets the ideas down where we can start revising: changing, adding, chopping.

There are also "unblocking" strategies you can use to get yourself started:

—Try free association writing at first. Just write down everything that comes to mind about your subject, regardless of whether it makes any sense. When you've finished, search through that tangled weedpatch and you'll find some sentences you can actually use in your writing. Then start with them.

—Start writing the *second* paragraph of your piece. Openings are hard to write, and sometimes they scare writers off. Begin with the second paragraph—the "meat" of your story—and write the beginning later.

—Write words or phrases instead of whole sentences. You can fill in the missing syntax later.

—Dictate the opening of your paper to a parent or friend. Just tell them what you want to say and let them write it down for you. Or dictate to yourself by talking into a tape recorder, then copying down your own language.

—Write the ending first. Once you know how it ends, you may find it easier to write the part that leads up to it.

Once you get started, the writing often comes in a rush, and you'll find yourself trying to write as fast as you think, which isn't easy. (Learning to type helps, since most people can type much faster than they can write by hand.) As you write your first draft, don't worry about spelling, grammar, and punctuation. You can take care of those matters later. Don't pause in your writing to look up words or to worry over mechanics. When you're hot, you're hot; when you're writing, keep on writing.

(If you're concerned about mechanics, grammar, and usage, now might be a good time to read Chapter Nine, which deals with the process of revising and correcting your writing.)

Above all, as you draft, enjoy yourself. Even though writing is hard work, it is pleasurable, too, and it is a wonderful experience to see the ideas you've thought about for hours and days and even weeks take shape on the page. So, as writer Jesse Stuart has said: "Write to please yourself."*

---

*Jesse Stuart, from *Writing for Love or Money*, Norman Cousins, ed. (1949), and reprinted in Floyd Watkins and Carl Knight, *Writer to Writer: Readings on the Craft of Writing* (1966).

Letters as a Way to Get Things Done

5

We are fans of the post office. Although you hear a lot of complaints about the postal service—that it's too expensive, that it loses the mail—it seems to us that sending letters is one of the most efficient and enjoyable ways of communicating with other people. The postal service has come a long way since the days of the Pony Express, when riders on horseback carried mail pouches across the country on a risky and expensive ride. Sending the mail in those days was so costly only the wealthy could afford it, and then only on special occasions.

Today the "postage stamp express" is as close and convenient as your mailbox. For half the price of a can of pop you can send a letter anywhere in the U.S. or Canada, and for about twice that amount you can send a letter almost anywhere in the world. During the time we were drafting this chapter, we had occasion to send letters to Australia, New Zealand, South Africa, Great Britain, Canada (twice, once to Vancouver on the west coast, once to Ottawa in eastern Ontario), Alaska, Hawaii, Virginia, Texas, West Virginia, Kansas, Illinois, New York, Minnesota, and northern Michigan (this last one being sent almost five hundred miles from our home in southern Michigan). If we had used the phone to contact those same friends, we would have run up a monstrous phone bill. As it was, we spent less than six dollars on postage.

We also like the way letters allow us to think through and revise what we're going to say to people. One can be more thoughtful in letter writing than in improvising a conversation on the phone. We often write drafts of letters and think about them for a day before mailing them. More than once we've drafted an angry letter to someone, then, after a day, thought better of it and written something calmer and more rational.

We also enjoy receiving letters. Nothing beats the satisfaction of going to the mailbox and discovering that someone has written to you. "A letter," says poet Stephen Spender, "is like a present." You can reread a letter many times, savoring its contents, and letters provide a concrete record of what people have said to you (something especially useful when you're writing for business purposes).

However, if you want to receive letters, you have to initiate the process by sending some. We suggest that after you've read this chapter (or even *as* you're reading it), you start a letter-writing campaign. Plan to write a letter each day for a month. If that sounds too ambitious, try two letters a week for a month. By the time that month is up you'll find your mailbox filling regularly—the payoff will have begun. Keep on writing letters, and before long it will seem as if you're getting something interesting in the mail every day.

In the process of doing all this letter writing, by the way, you'll be sharpening your writing skills. Because you know there is an audience or readership for your letters, you'll be more precise and careful in your writing than you will if you are writing only for yourself. You can even use letters to get an audience for your creative writing, sending plays, poems, and stories to people who range from friends in distant cities to magazine editors.

We recommend that you organize right away to keep a record of your correspondence. Make carbon copies of letters you send to provide you with a copy of what you've said. When the replies come in, fasten them to the carbons. You can punch holes in the letters and carbons and keep them in a three-ring binder, or you can simply file correspondence in an empty box or carton. As your correspondence grows, you can invent some other ways of filing letters, perhaps clustering your mail to and from friends in one file, letters to and from relatives in another, business letters in a third file, and so on.

Delivering the Mail by Hand

Even though postage stamps are relatively inexpensive, you don't even have to use the postal service to get your letter writing campaign started. You can write notes and letters and deliver them by hand.

When we were kids—probably about seven or eight years old—we set up a "mail drop" with some of our neighborhood friends. We found an apple tree with a hollow in it and left notes for one another. You don't need an apple tree to start your own mail system, though. You can simply agree with a friend to leave notes and letters at some secret place: in your desks at school, in one another's lockers, slipped under someone's front door, dropped through the pet port, slipped into someone's lunch box. If you ever read spy novels, you know that espionage agents do this sort of thing all the time, calling it a "dead letter drop" and leaving packages, notes, film canisters, and whatnot at prearranged locations.

(Note: Don't leave your hand-delivered mail in your friend's actual mailbox; that's a violation of postal service regulations.)

Around town, you can hand deliver your business or practical correspondence as well. If you write to local businesses, colleges, government agencies, and community experts (as we'll suggest later in this chapter), you can hop on your bike and deliver your mail for free.

You may also be able to set up some sort of hand-delivered mail system in your school. Just as your class in elementary school probably had a Valentine's Day mailbox, you can make a mailbox for day-to-day correspondence. If your teacher likes the idea, you might even write a letter to your local postmaster asking for suggestions on how to set up a school mail system. You might think that the postal service would disapprove of hand-delivered systems because of competition, but they have some useful publications explaining how to do it. (Their purpose is to help people your age better understand how the mail system works.) The postmaster may even be willing to come to your class to explain how to do it or to arrange for a guided tour of the post office so you can see how the pros manage the mail.

Nor does hand-delivered mail have to be limited to your immediate neighborhood or your hometown. If you know people who commute to another city, you may be able to have them deliver notes to your friends there, either in person or through a dead letter drop at a prearranged location. We know of an elementary school class that "hand delivered" mail by balloon! They wrapped letters in plastic sandwich bags and tied them to helium balloons. The balloons were released into the wind, were carried long distances, but eventually came down. People who found the letters then wrote back to the class (using the postal service, not balloons, by the way). We know, too, of a man who lives on an island and sends off letters by kite, fastening letters to the string, adding just the right number of weights, and letting the kites fly by themselves. No doubt you can think of some other clever ways to deliver the mail to distant places.

Writing Friendly Letters

Letters are usually divided into two categories: "friendly" letters sent to friends and acquaintances, mostly to catch them up on news about your life and to learn what's happening to them, and business or "practical" letters sent to companies, government, universities, and other institutions seeking information or transacting business. We'll begin with friendly letters in this section, so get yourself a stack of writing paper or stationery, some envelopes, and start writing.

(Note: Part of the pleasure in friendly writing can come from making your own writing paper using plain or colored paper and hand-drawn or stamped decorations and monograms. You can also make your own postcards, which deliver a message by mail more cheaply than a letter. We've described how to do this in another book published by Charles Scribner's Sons, *Gifts of Writing.*)

Letters to Friends and Relatives. Even though delivering mail by hand is enjoyable, we're going to guess that before long you'll want to use the regular postal service for friendly letters, if only because it lets you get in touch with people who live far away.

Pen Pals. When you run out of people you know, you may be ready to start a pen pal correspondence, writing to a stranger who is soon to become your friend. You might be able to get the name of a pen pal from a next-door neighbor, who could suggest the names of nieces, nephews, and grandchildren in other cities. Your teacher may be able to supply other names; in fact, your class might start a pen pal exchange of letters with a school in another part of the country. (We recently heard of schools that have become pen pals by computer, with the students mailing one another, not paper letters, but computer floppy disks. Students read their mail on the computer's TV monitor.)

It's easy to get pen pals in other countries, too. Here are several organizations the postal service lists in its publications. To get the name of a pen pal, you will generally have to pay a small fee, something between fifty cents and two dollars. You can request a pen pal in a specific country, and some organizations will even supply a pen pal who will write to you in another language you may be studying. For information, write:

League of Friendship, Inc., P. O. Box 509, Mt. Vernon, Ohio 43050.

International Friendship League, Inc., 22 Batterymarch, Boston, Massachusetts 02109.

Student Letter Exchange, 910 Fourth Street S.E., Austin, Minnesota 55912.

World Pen Pals, 1690 Como Avenue, St. Paul, Minnesota 55108.

When you write to your pen pal for the first time, do a good job of introducing yourself, including:

—What you look like. (Include photo.)

—Where you live.

—Your family.

—Your friends.

—Information about school.

—Information about hobbies, sports, etc.

—Descriptions of favorites (food, music, books, films).

—Stories about yourself (funny, odd, good times, bad times).

Remember that if you are writing to a person in another country, your pen pal may not know very much about American customs and traditions. Don't start talking about Thanksgiving or Frisbees or even football or rock 'n' roll without explaining what those traditions and customs are like.

When you are ready to mail your letter to a foreign pen pal, go to the post office and have your letter weighed. The postal clerk will tell you how much postage you need. Although it is more expensive, use overseas *air mail* rather than *surface mail*. Air mail will get your letter there in a week, while surface mail may literally take months. When your pen pal replies, send a letter back quickly so your correspondence does not grow cold.

Letters to Shut-Ins and the Elderly. Consider developing a "pen pal" relationship with an elderly person or a shut-in. To get the name of a person to write, telephone a home for the elderly or ask the leaders at your church or YMCA.

At first you may feel a little awkward writing to an older pen pal. Treat him or her as you would a friend: Start out by introducing yourself; then ask your pen pal to tell you something about him or herself. Invite the person to share memories and stories with you by asking about his/her past experiences. If your pen pal lives close by, you may want to supplement your writing with personal visits. But don't forget to write; it's one of the most valuable gifts you can give.

Letters and Cards on Special Occasions. Americans send millions and millions of cards on birthdays, anniversaries, Christmas, Chanukah, Easter, Passover, Valentine's Day, Mother's Day, Father's Day, and so on. Although it's nice to send a store-bought card, consider writing letters or short notes or even making your own greeting cards on these occasions. When you take time to write a personal note or letter, people know you *really* care enough to send the very best.

Letters can also be sent instead of commercial cards on sad occasions. A person who has been ill or who has experienced the death of a loved one may especially appreciate your hand-written note. Don't feel nervous about writing on such occasions or feel that you can't refer directly to the illness or death. Write down what you are truly feeling about your friend's difficult times.

Fan Mail. Do you drool over the handsome hero's manly biceps? Are you in love with the heroine of a prime time TV show? Have you read a new book that you think is the greatest work of literature since Shakespeare? Have you listened to a recent album so many times you've worn out the grooves?

Consider writing fan mail to your favorite TV, literary, film, radio, or recording personality. You can probably guess that your fan mail is not likely to bring you a long and detailed reply of the sort you will receive from your friends. A star may send you an autographed photo, a printed thank-you, or nothing at all. Still, writing fan letters is a way of letting people know you appreciate their work and admire what they are doing. Further, some writers and stars answer their fan mail faithfully, so you may get the surprise and excitement of a personal letter back.

To send fan mail to a television star, you can often write to the network that sponsors the program. (For the addresses of the four major networks in the U.S.A., see the next section of this chapter.) For recording stars, look for the address of the record company on the album jacket. Letters to authors can be sent care of their publishers, whose addresses usually appear up front in a book. For a film star, you'll need to learn the name of the company that produced the film (check a film ad in the newspaper or a poster at the theater). If you have trouble finding an address, ask for help at your library, where the librarian has a variety of resources to assist you.

Writing Practical Letters

In business and government, time is scarce and people don't have a lot of time to spend in idle chatter.

"Send me a memo about it."

"Put your thoughts in writing."

"Let me have a memorandum summarizing your progress."

"We'll confirm this by letter."

Letters, notes, and memoes are a practical way to get things done in the world because they are short and to the point. Moreover, they're permanent, providing a record of what people have agreed to do.

Letter writing is a useful way of letting you communicate with people in business and government whom you cannot meet face to face. To take an extreme example, it's almost impossible to get in to see the President of the United States. However, if you write to the President, you'll get a reply back, if not from the President, at least from a member of the White House staff, and if not a personal letter, at least a printed acknowledgement. To take an example closer to home, in your own town it may be difficult to see someone like the mayor, but a letter will get you a reading and a response. You can use letter writing, then, to get your opinion across to people who would otherwise be out of reach.

The form of the practical or business letter is more formal than that of the friendly letter. (See Figure 6.) Note that you always include a return address in a practical letter, and you should write the address of the business firm or agency at the top of the letter. Unless you know the person on a first-name basis, stick to Mr., Mrs., Ms., Dr., or To Whom It May Concern in writing the greeting. The complimentary closing is more formal, too, usually "Yours truly" or " Sincerely yours" rather than a casual closing like "So long." In the good old days, over one hundred years ago, elaborate formal closings were appropriate, such as: "Your humble and obedient servant, I am, . . ." We rather wish those days would come back, but for now, keep those closings plain and simple.

Type your practical letters if you can. Otherwise, write them in your best penmanship, remembering that the recipient may get and read dozens (or even hundreds) of letters every day. Also, *triple*check your practical letters for correct spelling, usage, and grammar as a way of ensuring you'll make a good impression.

Letters to Radio and Television Stations. So . . . you're watching your favorite program and suddenly the hero does something totally out of character, like pushing an old lady out of line or being rude to his girlfriend. Or you're listening to the radio and a disc jockey says he won't play a new hit song because it makes him sick to his stomach, and the song happens to be your favorite. Or you're watching a TV movie that scares your younger brother or sister half to death and you find yourself saying, "Hey, they shouldn't show stuff like that at an hour when little kids are still up."

So what do you do?

You pick up your pen and write, sending a letter to the station expressing your opinion. You might not think that would do much good, but radio and TV stations do pay attention to what people write. In fact, the Federal Communications Commission—the outfit that gives out broadcasting licenses—requires stations to keep letters like yours on file.

To send a letter to a local station, look in the telephone book Yellow or White Pages under *Radio* or *Television Broadcasting*. If you want to write to one of the major television networks (the people who do most of the prime-time television shows), use one of these addresses:

NBC-TV, 30 Rockefeller Plaza, New York, NY 10020.

ABC-TV, 1330 Avenue of the Americas, New York, NY 10019.

CBS-TV, 51 West 52nd Street, New York, NY 10009.

Public Broadcasting Service, 425 L'Enfant Plaza S.W., Washington, D.C. 20024.

Letters to the Editor. Most newspapers and magazines have a letters column in which readers can express their opinions. If you have an idea about goings-on around your school or city, write to the editor of the appropriate paper airing your view. If you have an idea about an issue or topic discussed in your favorite magazine, write the editor a letter.

Begin this project by reading some letters in other issues of the paper or magazine; that will give you a sense of what people write about and how long the letters run. Keep your letter concise and tightly organized. Preplan by jotting down notes indicating the important points you want to make. Be specific, and include an example or two of what you're praising or complaining about. Write a rough draft, revise it, read it to a friend, and revise again. Finally, when you've gotten your letter honed and polished the way you want, make a clean final copy.

To find the name of the editor and the address of the publication, look for a box of fine print information near the table of contents in magazines, close to the editorial page in newspapers. Make certain you follow any special instructions about length, form of the letter, and contents. Some newspapers and magazines will ask you to include your phone number so the editor can call you up and confirm your opinion.

Then keep an eye on the publication for the next several issues to see if your letter is one of those accepted for publication. If your letter is printed, you should be prepared to see it edited—probably shortened—when it actually appears. Editors generally reserve the right to make changes without discussing them first with the letter writer. Also be prepared for a lot of public recognition when people see you've had a letter published in a newspaper or magazine.

Using Letters to Get Free Publicity. Suppose your school is having a fair or carnival as a fund-raising activity. Or your scout troop is having a pancake supper. Or your YMCA club is conducting a paper or aluminum can drive. You can use letters to get free publicity in newspapers and on radio and television.

Make up a short announcement describing the event you are sponsoring, including:

—Date, time, and place.

—Who's invited to participate.

—How much it costs, if anything.

—Whom people should contact for further information.

—Anything else you think is necessary.

Duplicate as many of the announcements as you need to send one to every newspaper and media station in town (check the Yellow or White Pages for addresses). Then write a series of short, individual letters to the business manager or the community service editor of each station asking them to read your announcement on the air or to print it in the paper. Ordinarily you'll need to get the announcement to the media at least three weeks before the event to get this very helpful free publicity.

Writing to Businesses. Millions of letters go to businesses and industry every day. People write to order products, to complain about products that perform poorly, to ask questions about how things work or why they don't work, and all too infrequently (from the point of view of those in business) to praise a company for the way a product works or for a stand the company has taken.

Writing the Government and Tax-Supported Institutions. There are hundreds of government offices and public institutions where you can write for information or to express your ideas, so many that we'll simply list the possibilities and let you think of what to write about. Many of these addresses can be obtained from your local phone book. For out-of-town offices (say, the state government), ask your parents, a librarian, or your teacher to help you find addresses.

Places and people to write:

—the mayor.

—the parks department.

—the fire and police departments.

—your school district or school board.

—the county agent.

—the governor.

—your state senator or representative.

—the departments of: natural resources, history, public information, commerce, aeronautics, animal health, farming, fishery, Indian and minority affairs, transportation.

—the President (The White House, Washington, D.C. 20500).

—your U.S. senator (Senate Office Building, Washington, D.C. 20515).

—your U.S. congresspeople (House of Representatives, Washington, D.C. 20515).

—museums (local history museums, school or county museums, national museums such as the Smithsonian in Washington, D.C.).

—libraries (school, local, state, the Library of Congress).

—colleges and universities (community, state, or private).

Making Practical Letters Effective

There are many dos and don'ts about writing effective letters to business and government, but most of them are just common sense and boil down to these two points:

First, make your letters as short as you can while still getting your point across.

Second, through your language and content, show people that you are someone to be taken seriously.

Some other things to keep in mind:

1. *Know what you're writing about.* If you are writing about a malfunctioning product, make certain you have followed the instructions exactly and tested the gizmo two or three times. If you're writing for information, make certain you state your questions clearly. If you are writing to express an opinion, be certain you have read about or studied the topic so your observation is an intelligent one.

2. *Think about your opinion or ideas before writing.* What exactly do you want to say? It's a good idea with practical letters to write a rough draft. In fact, it may even prove useful for you to write a journal entry before you do your draft.

3. *Put yourself in your reader's shoes.* The person who will get your letters is human, too. Thus, don't write, "I think your product stinks." Or, "What are you guys, a bunch of crooks?" Consider your readers and their feelings and be polite and courteous in tone. (That doesn't mean you have to pull your punches and not say what's on your mind; just say it politely.)

4. *Follow business letter form and make your copy readable.* Make sure your grammar, spelling, and punctuation are correct.

5. *Doublecheck to make certain you have the right address.*

If you become skilled at writing business letters, you'll find it has a practical pay off in many parts of your life. Not only will you be able to use that skill now, but it will prove invaluable to you later, say, when you're applying for a job or for college.

Figure 6   *The Form of the Practical Letter*

Every practical or business letter should include the following:

Return Address. Written or typed in the upper right corner.
The Date. Written directly beneath the return address. Dates are especially important in business letters.
The Address. Type out or write the full address here, exactly as it will appear on the envelope.
The Greeting. It used to be that if you didn't know a person, you wrote, "My Dear _____Name_____." Nowadays "Dear" will suffice. Don't write anything cutesy like "Hi there" or "Howdy Folks." If a person has a title, use it in the greeting: "Dear Senator Foghorn," "Dear Dr. Jeckyl."
The Body. Your message, stated as clearly and concisely as possible.
The Complimentary Closing. Use "Yours truly" or "Sincerely yours."
Your Signature and Name. Sign your name, then print or type it again for clarity.

Figure 6 *(continued)*

THE LETTER

Return Address xxxxxx
xxxxxxxxxxxxxxxxxxxxx
xxxxxxxxxxxxxxxxx Zip
Date xxxxxxxxxxxxxxx

Address xxxxxxxxxxxxx
xxxxxxxxxxxxxxxxxxxxx
xxxxxxxxxxxxxxxxx Zip

Greeting,

Body of letter xxxxxxxxxxxxxxxxxxxxxxxxxxxxxxxxxxxxxxxxxx
xxxxxxxxxxxxxxxxxxxxxxxxxxxxxxxxxxxxxxxxxxxxxxxxxxxxxxx

xxxxxxxxxxxxxxxxxxxxxxxxxxxxxxxxxxxxxxxxxxxxxxxxxxxxxxx
xxxxxxxxxxxxxxxxxxxxxxxxxxxxxxxxxxxxxxxxxxxxxxxxxxxxx

Complimentary closing,

Signature

Your name

THE ENVELOPE

Your return address xxxxxxxx
xxxxxxxxxx xxxxxxxxxxxxxxxxx
xxxxxxxxxxxxxxxxxxxxxxxxxx Zip

Stamp

Address xxxxxxxxxxxxxxxxxxxxxxxxxxxx
xxxxxxxxxxxxxxxxxxxxxxxxxxxxxxxxxx
xxxxxxxxxxxxxxxxxxxxxxxxxxxxxxxxx Zip

A MEMORANDUM

July 31, 1983

TO: The Readers of This Book
FROM: The Authors
REGARDING: Memoranda

A memorandum (or simply "memo") is a short way to send a business note to another person without the formality of addresses and greetings. You would send a memo only to a person with whom you are working regularly and who knows your address. Memos are very convenient and handy for those purposes. Try sending some.

Writing Fiction, Plays, and Poems

6

Writing Fiction

You are already a storyteller.

You like to tell stories about what's happening to you and around you. You tell your parents about what happened in school: Mr. Jones yelled at you for leaving your homework in your locker; Eddie stole Andy's lunch and got sent to the office; Sandy's mother won't let her attend sex education class. You exchange stories with your friends: Mr. Marco kicked Ray off the swim team; Mrs. Vincent is leaving teaching to go to law school; Andrea's parents are getting a divorce; you're in trouble with your parents for leaving your bike out in the rain. You tell stories not only about what's happening to you now, but about things that have happened to you and others in the past. You reminisce with family and friends about experiences you shared. You become better acquainted with people by sharing your past.

Many of the stories you tell have the potential for becoming fiction—short stories or even a novel. Some events will make a good story if you retell them just as they happened. Others can provide the basis for a story that "takes off" from the event or episode and assumes a life of its own.

Whether you are telling a story as fiction or nonfiction, the essential literary element is *plot*, which simply means a story line or story idea. Each of the episodes we mentioned has the potential to become a good plot, because each has the essential ingredient of a good story line: a *conflict* or a problem to be resolved. For example, even though Eddie was accused of stealing Andy's lunch, Eddie swears he didn't do it. A written story plot would center on resolving that conflict or problem. In the case of Mr. Marco, the whole swim team might think that Ray was unjustly kicked off the team. "Was Mr. Marco right or wrong?" a story will ask. "What will the team do about it?" Perhaps you could create a written story from the time you left your bike in the rain. Here is a good opportunity to fictionalize your experience. Rather than having the character's parents angry because the bike was left in the rain (as it happened in real life), you might pretend that the bike was stolen due to the character's carelessness in not locking it. Now her folks are *really* angry.

In deciding whether to turn an event or experience into a story, think about how intriguing and interesting you can make the problem or conflict. Is it one that people care about, one that will keep their interest and make them want to see it solved or resolved?

In addition to a dramatic or engaging problem, you will need to have an interesting solution. In the case of the missing bike, you would want to have a more dramatic solution than simply having the character find it on the street. Perhaps she could learn that a good friend was involved in stealing bicycles; should she turn that friend in to the authorities? In the case of the swim team, perhaps the whole team refuses to participate in the meet only to find out later that Mr. Marco had information about the teammate that he wasn't willing to reveal even if it meant having to forfeit the meet.

Just as you can use your experiences as a jumping off point for your fictional stories, so can you use real people as the starting point for characters. In Chapter Four we suggested that you list some people in your life and people in whom you are interested. Each of those folks could be modeled in one of your stories. However, if you start with a real person as the basis for your story, you must be willing to change that character so he or she fits the purpose of the story. For example, if you are using your brother as a model, you may get to a point in your writing where a character needs to take certain action your brother would never take. You need to be will-

79   Writing Fiction, Plays, and Poems

ing to make the character "work" in terms of the story rather than sticking to the model for the character.

Sometimes you'll read at the beginning of a novel, "Any resemblance between characters portrayed in this work of fiction and real people is strictly coincidental." That statement protects the writer from being sued by a person who might think he or she is the model for the character and then doesn't like what the character does in the novel. In many cases, there may be a more than coincidental resemblance between a real person and a character in fiction, but because a writer changes the character to fit the story, he or she is justified in saying to readers: "This is fiction, not real life. Any resemblance is coincidental."

One reason it is helpful to use actual people as models is that you are more likely to create "realistic" characters. Even when you don't model a character on a specific person, your knowledge of people helps you with characterization. Avoid using stereotyped characters such as the hardened cop, the dizzy waitress, the unredeemable criminal. Make your characters have complex personalities. Instead of a dumb athlete, create a football player who is good at school as well as being talented on the field; instead of the stereotypical smart kid with thick glasses, create a smart kid who defies the clichés and lifts weights in his basement; instead of a housewife mother who meets kids at the door with milk and cookies, create a mother who's a criminal lawyer. Let "bad" characters have "good" qualities, too, and let your heroes and heroines have some flaws. In short, have your characters be like authentic people rather than cartoon characters.

After you have a problem or story line or plot idea and you've settled on some main characters, you will need to decide who is going to tell your story. Your *narrator* may be one of the characters in the story, in which case you will have a *first person* narrator, someone who uses "I" and "we" and is a part of the tale him- or herself. The character may be a relatively minor part of the plot, someone who views events as an outsider, or he or she may be the major character who is telling about his/her experiences:

I live in a huge old house with my mother and our three dogs—English sheep dogs. My mom says that the house is over a hundred years old. To me it looks as if it's a thousand years old. The paint is peeling off inside and out. My mom says I get to help paint it. Terrific.

If you use a first person narrator, you will only be able to tell the story from that person's perspective. You must be careful *not* to tell about events that the narrator could not possibly have known about. Moreover, you will not be able to go inside the minds of other characters to tell what they are thinking or feeling.

A *third person narrator* writes from outside the story, talking about "he," "she," and "they," not "I" and "we." Sometimes the narrator will relate the story from one character's point of view, as if standing behind that character and seeing everything over his/her shoulder or through his/her eyes:

John was discouraged. He thought about how hard he had worked all year, how many practices he had attended, about all the help he had gotten from his tennis teacher, about how happy his parents were he was trying out for the team. He couldn't believe he had been cut from the squad.

Another kind of narrator—an *omniscient* narrator—can get into the minds of all the characters and tell the reader what they are thinking:

John's father could see in his son's face that he hadn't made the team, but he didn't want to be the first one to bring it up. He didn't want to make John talk about it before he was ready. Mrs. Ferguson wasn't so patient. She'd been waiting for John to come home all day, and she couldn't go through dinner with all the tension in the air.
Well, here goes, she thought. "John, what happened about the tennis team?"

As you write your story, concentrate on recreating the scenes and events so your readers will feel they are there. One way to do that is through your use of physical description. Your reader should be able to visualize your characters, the surroundings, the action. Compare these two passages.

> When Pam arrived at school, she went to the bike racks, and her heart sank. Her bike was not among those in the rack. Pam was depressed and nervous when she thought about what her parents would say.

○ ○ ○ ○

> As Pam left school, she hurried her pace, and by the time she reached the edge of the library, she was running. She turned the corner of the library onto the path that led to the bike rack. From the end of the building, she could see there were six or seven bikes, but they blended into one another, so she couldn't make out their features. There was a blue one, she could see, and she went to it. But a few feet from the rack, she realized it wasn't hers. Her eyes went over the bikes again. Hers wasn't there. She had known deep inside that she hadn't locked it, and she knew it was gone, probably for good. She heard her father's voice in her head: "Pamela, I paid good money for that bike, only to have you treat it as if you didn't care."
>   She started to cry.

In the second passage, rather than simply telling the reader that the bike was gone, the storyteller helps the reader see and feel Pam making the discovery. And the writer helps you feel her reaction. Rather than simply telling you that Pam felt depressed, the writer has shown you her father's anticipated reaction.

Though you might want to have physical descriptions of the characters in the story, it often works better to integrate those descriptions into the action. The following passages advance the story and tell you what the character and the surroundings look like:

> Sarah couldn't believe that her parents would really get a divorce. As she felt the tears start to come into her eyes, she threw herself on her canopy bed, the beautiful bed her father had made for her tenth birthday.

○ ○ ○

Coach Marco stood before the angry faces of his team. His face was tired and pale, but he was angry. The guys knew he was thirty-five. Somehow, when he was furious like this, he looked forty-five.

Rather than using a separate paragraph, you can include details about the place or people in your story, telling and showing what they looked like as the story flows along.

Dialog is a useful way to bring a story to life. In Chapter Three we suggested that you write samples of conversation in your journal. That sort of recording skill will come in handy when you tell stories, because you will be better able to characterize people through their conversations.

One of the biggest problems with dialog, though, is making clear who is talking. The simplest way, of course, is to write, "Sarah said," "Mother said," and so on. The trouble is, that becomes boring if you have a long conversation, and pretty soon you run out of synonyms for "said," words like "replied," "agreed," "disagreed," "argued."

A solution to that problem is to include information about your characters just before or after they speak. That way you can leave out the "hesaids" and "shesaids":

> "All right, guys, what seems to be the problem?" Mr. Marco was giving them his stern look.
> John's voice was quiet, soft. "Well, Mr. Marco. We kinda think Ray should be back on the team."
> Rick was more forceful and direct. "Tell us why he's off, Coach. At least you owe us that."
> Mr. Marco shrugged, looking sad. "Sorry, guys. I just can't do that."

Above all, as you write, let your story tell itself. If you've thought beforehand about the conflict or problem, if you've considered carefully what you want your characters to be like, this will happen. Novelists regularly describe the experience of having a story take over and write itself, and we suspect you will experience the same thing. Pretty soon Pam, the victim of bicycle theft, becomes a new person, a character other than you (who merely left a bicycle out in the rain), and Pam will live through your storytelling. Or you'll find yourself so involved in writing the swim team story that when Mr. Marco shrugs off the boys, you'll find yourself getting angry. That's a good sign that your fiction is truly realistic, and a good sign that it will engage your readers.

Thus far we've written about realistic fiction, but that's not the only kind you might want to try. *Fantasy* and *science fiction* are two other popular forms of storytelling. One way to get started on a good fantasy/sf story is to ask, "What if . . . ?"

For example, what would happen if . . .

—there were a whole, complete, separate world in the center of the earth?

—babies suddenly had the power of mental telepathy?

—the sun started perceptibly losing its power?

—cats suddenly started to double in size?

—there were a nuclear war?

—scientists found the key to eternal life?

—all babies were made in test tubes?

Use your imagination to develop the general situation for your fantasy/sf story. Begin by describing the details of the event: Who discovers it? How does word get out? How do people react? What action is proposed to solve the problem? After you have developed the basic pattern for your story, then develop characters and the problems they would face in this "what if" situation. Even though your story will not be "real" in the strictest sense, it will be important for you to create a believable story so readers care about and are affected by it.

Myths are traditional stories from ancient cultures that described phenomena in nature before there were scientific explanations. You can create your own myths explaining such things as why leaves fall off the trees, what makes hailstones, how Niagara Falls or Old Faithful were created, or what set off the Mount St. Helens volcano. You can also create myths for our modern world: What (or who) makes the treads on sneakers? Where does aluminum come from? How are charcoal briquets made? How does a lawnmower cut grass? Your story can make any explanation you choose, ranging from the work of gods and goddesses (like many ancient myths) to unknown weather forces, to little creatures too small for humans to see, to outer space beings. Here your purpose will be to create detailed and convincing explanations—or at least, if not convincing, funny enough to make your reader laugh.

Detective and *mystery stories* are also constructed around a problem, but in this case the problem is usually a crime and the solution must reveal the answer to the classic question, "Whodunnit?" Suspense and the desire to know what's going to happen, how the problem will be solved, and what the solution will be are intensified in the mystery story. To keep the suspense going you will need to provide clues and complications throughout the story. The good mystery provides several possibilities for how the crime was committed and who did the committing. Some discoveries by the detective may be real clues, but some may be false leads for both the detective and the reader. To play fair in writing a story, however, in the end your clues should lead to one, and only one, solution to the problem. Also it's not "fair" to withhold information from the reader so he or she can't solve the crime.

There are other types of fiction you might enjoy writing—the romance, the western, historical fiction, the horror story. If you haven't already, you'll want to do some reading of the kind of fiction you are interested in writing. As you read, you'll "soak up" the conventions of the genre and learn some of the tricks of the trade that authors use.

No matter what type of fiction you choose to write, your experiences in life so far will be the basis for your work. Even if you are writing about something remote or imaginary, things as distant as the Civil War or the year 3000, what you have done, read, thought about, and explored will serve as the background from which you write. In that way, even though they are made up, your fiction stories will be true.

Writing Plays

In order to write a good play, you need two essential elements: The first is a problem or conflict that will be resolved during the course of the play; the second is a set of interesting characters who have this problem or conflict. Sound familiar? These are precisely the elements that make a good piece of fiction. The central difference is that in writing a play, you must contain all the action in one place (the stage) and reveal all the development through dialog or conversation. A play is essentially a story acted out.

As with fiction writing, your own experience is a good starting point for coming up with the central conflict of a drama. It can be a conflict between two people or within a central character. The conflict or problem need not be an earthshaking one. Many of the problems that you face in your day-to-day life can be the stuff of good drama. You could write a play about:

—Janice, who has agreed to babysit for some friends who trust only her with their infant. She then discovers that her class has scheduled a trip to a theme park the same day.

—Mike, whose friend Tim finds it easier to borrow homework than to do it himself, to the point that Mike feels he is being taken advantage of and his teachers are accusing him of cheating.

—Mary, who borrowed her sister's heirloom necklace without permission and then lost it. (Or was it stolen?)

Conflicts with parents can provide good ideas for plays:

—Doug, who wants to go to a rock concert. Unfortunately, the concert is in a town fifty miles away. Fortunately, Doug's friend's older brother is going to go and has agreed to drive. Unfortunately, Doug's parents don't approve of the big brother. . . .

Another source of writing ideas for plays can be values and beliefs. What you believe to be important might be reflected in some old sayings:

"Haste makes waste."

"Honesty is the best policy."

"Money is the root of all evil."

Think about the beliefs you hold as important, then think about a situation in which those values might be challenged, threatened, or questioned. You might have a situation in your own life that you can draw upon, or you might want to fictionalize your experiences. You might, for example, write a play about:

—Miriam, who discovers that whether she does her homework "quick and dirty" or slowly and carefully, she gets the same grades. *Does* haste make waste?

—Jack, who finds a large sum of money and tries to return it to its rightful owner, only to be accused of having stolen it. *Is* honesty the best policy?

—Jane, who inherits a sum of money from an aunt she never knew she had and uses it to finance her college education. *Is* money the root of all evil?

In addition to having a central conflict, your play needs interesting characters who must be more than mere cardboard figures. The people need to be different from one another: one frivolous and giggly (but not stereotyped), another studious and reserved, a third frank and outspoken, a fourth bossy, a fifth flirtatious. Let those aspects of character be revealed as the people interact with one another.

Again, remember to keep your characters full-dimensioned and realistic. Silly people have their serious moments; reserved people can be witty; outspoken characters can become shy; bossy people sometimes meet their match. Try to make the characters of your play like real people with complex attitudes and personalities. Using real people as models might help you create well-rounded characters, and your writing of fiction and nonfiction can be helpful here, since both require accurate portrayals of people.

In stories and novels, the narrator is able to tell the audience what to think of a character through descriptions of personality, dress, gesture, language, and physical appearance. Although the playwright can give some of this kind of information through stage directions, the audience will gain most of its information through the talk of the characters. You'll have to use language as a way of revealing personality as well as moving the plot along.

Think about the language of people you know or have met. Notice how, for example, the language of an aggressive person differs from that of a shy person. In preparing to write dialog, listen for the language characteristic of the flirt, the wit, the scholar, the jock, the boss, the parent, the female, the male, the worker, the teacher, the child. Look for differences in what these people talk about as well as in the form and style of their language.

When you first begin to write your play, you may have only a general idea of what you want to have happen. Just as it is with fiction, writing drama is a process of discovery, and sometimes your characters and plot will take on a life of their own and the play will end in a way different from that originally planned. Even if you don't have all the fine details of your play worked out, plunge ahead; your indecision will be resolved as you write.

Here are some things to keep in mind as you write:

—Keep the play moving, in more than one sense of the word. Make certain there is plenty of action: people coming and going, events taking place. A play that features two people sitting around talking can be dull. TV soap operas offer a good example here, because something happens every few minutes, keeping the action rolling along.

—Use minor characters from time to time. You can use these people to introduce new elements into the plot or to carry information on stage. Within limits, adding characters also adds to the interest of the play.

—Don't change scenes too often. Young playwrights often have a change of scene (and scenery) every few pages or so, and that makes for an impractical production. Concentrate on what the classical Greek dramatists called "unity of place" and figure out ways to have most of your action take place in a single location.

—Introduce minor conflicts or subplots from time to time. Although "honesty is the best policy" may be the central theme of your play, you might have a love subplot or one centering around the hero(ine)'s relationship with his/her parents.

—Make certain the ending of the play is in keeping with the traits of the characters. That is, keep all your characters consistent throughout the play. If your hero *wouldn't* tell a lie, don't have him fib at the end. If your heroine is not the crying type, don't have her blubbering as the curtain goes down. Often, however, the end of the play will bring about growth in the characters, so they aren't the same people as they were when the play started.

—Beware of endings that are *deus ex machina*, which is Latin for "god from a machine." In certain Greek and Roman dramas, the conflicts were resolved by having one of the gods descend from the skies, perhaps to save the hero. This descending was done by hooking an actor to a rope and pulley (a machine) and lowering him to the stage. The phrase has come to stand for an ending in which all problems are suddenly, unexpectedly, and magically cleared up. So be cautious about an ending where a) a long lost brother turns up to save the day, b) the whole thing turns out to be a bad dream, c) the police show up unexpectedly and just in the nick of time, d) anything happens for which you have not prepared your audience.

—Though you may prefer happy endings, your solution to the conflict need not be one in which all of the characters end up getting what they want. The most effective ending will be true-to-life and leave your audience with something to think about.

We mentioned that *stage directions* are a way for a writer to talk, indirectly, to the audience and the actors. Good stage directions can make a great difference in whether or not your play comes alive and works for an audience. The first set of stage directions will be the list of characters, accompanied by a brief description of the character:

Josie, a thirteen-year-old girl, still somewhat childlike, but cheerful and outgoing.

Don, her older brother, sixteen, serious, and very mature.

The cast of characters is followed by a brief description of the time and the place where the play occurs:

The entire play takes place in the middle 1980s in a small town in Ohio.

Next is a description of the set, which essentially tells a reader how to imagine the scenes and tells a director how to arrange the furniture and the props. (In theater language, *stage right* and *left* refer to the actor's right and left as he faces the audience. *Downstage* is toward the front of the stage; *upstage* is toward the back.)

The entire play takes place in the Tylers' living room. It is a plain but comfortable room. The front door is stage left and there is an entrance to the dining room stage right. A large picture window covered with chintz curtains is in the center. Downstage center is a comfortable-looking stuffed sofa with a battered coffee table in front of it covered with magazines.

The first lines in the play itself will probably be stage directions, too, getting everything rolling:

Jane enters stage right with a cup of coffee and a newspaper in her hand. She sits on the sofa, sets down her coffee, and begins to read. Don enters quietly, looking for something.

Information about characters' responses and movements is entered as dialog begins, thus:

DON: (*looking at the coffee table, couch*) Have you seen my math homework?

JANE: (*not looking up from the paper*) No. Never saw it.

Good stage directions will greatly assist your readers and your director in understanding the intent of your play.

As you can see, writing a play is complex and time-consuming work.

You'll probably be surprised that pages and pages of script sometimes turn out to be only a few minutes of action on the stage. You'll learn, too, of some of the complications of play writing, complications induced by the fact that you have all the action limited to the stage and by the fact that you have to indicate so much through dialog. At the same time, when you've successfully written a play, you will have created a unique literary and art form, one that almost demands being presented, either read aloud or acted. When you've put the finishing touches on your script, round up a cast of your friends and say, "Hey, folks, let's put on a play."

Writing Poems

Sometimes people feel that poetry has to be about monumental human questions like WHAT IS TRUTH? WHAT IS BEAUTY? WHAT IS THE MEANING OF LIFE? Though poetry often gives insight into those matters, most good poetry does it through poets' giving visions of their worlds, their *particular* worlds.

Anything can be the subject of a poem: hating beets or being late for school, your kitten rolling on the carpet, stubbing your toe running up the stairs, getting your hair cut, snow melting off your roof and forming an icicle, a plant wilting from too much sun, seeing the last out in an important game. Here are two poems about rather ordinary experiences, the first by Millicent Brower:

down by the brook

down by the brook
hot skies at noon
I take off
my sneaker, my sock

my big toe
wriggles first
into the crystal stream

my other toes
follow
wriggling too

feeling
the soothing lap
of the tiny waves

I know
what it is like
to be wet moss
on a rock

or a new-born guppy
exploring
the cool waters
for the first time°

The second is by Stephen Tchudi:

The Thing

It came from another planet,
Crash landed on the Arctic icepack,
And was frozen in a block of ice.

Scientists, inquisitive,
Dragged the icy thing
To their quarters
And wondered what to do next.

The thing decided for them.
At ten P.M. (by the moviehouse clock)
It thawed free and
Killed every scientist within reach.

For months afterward
(or maybe a day or two or only once),
I awoke from my sleep hollering
At ten P.M. sharp.

°Millicent Brower, "down by the brook," in *The Scribner Anthology for Young People*, Anne Diven, ed. (1976).

Both of those poems are about experiences you might have had—dangling your feet in the water or being scared by a horror movie. The poet brings to life feelings we have felt and reminds us of similar events in our lives.

Poetry is often restricted in what it tries to cover. Although you might someday write an *epic* poem like *The Odyssey*, a poem that retells all the adventures of the Greek hero, Odysseus, usually you will focus your poem on a specific experience or moment. Instead of trying to talk about all horror shows or the feeling of being afraid, the poet took one specific movie and described a single incident of being frightened into wakefulness. And rather than writing in broad terms about summer and water and what lives in water, the poet brought to life a single moment of foot-dangling.

Poetry captures small experiences in a compact and vivid way, so readers can see and feel what the poet has seen or done or experienced. In just a few words, the poet can give you new insights into something familiar and ordinary or can touch off emotions and recollections. In creating poems that have impact, you need to communicate both what you see (and hear and smell and touch and taste) and what you feel and think. Poet Ted Hughes emphasizes the importance of tuning into what you are writing about with all your senses, with your whole being:

> See it and live it. Do not think it up laboriously, as if you were working out mental arithmetic. Just look at it, touch it, smell it, listen to it, turn yourself into it.°

Poet Myra Cohn Livingston recommends the use of an observation sheet to help you capture both the experience and the feeling about that experience. She suggests dividing a sheet of paper and listing what you observe with your senses on one side and how you feel on the other.† We tried this:

°Ted Hughes, *Poetry Is* (1970).
†Myra Cohn Livingston, *When You Are Alone* (1973).

What I Saw	*What I Felt*
The deck with patches	moving back and forth from
of sunlight and patches	sun to shade to avoid getting
of shade on the wood.	too sweaty; drinking diet coke
The bar-b-que grill,	hardly moving.
with the black plastic	hot dogs with greasy grill marks
hood on top, waiting for	buns toasted in the smoke
another picnic.	I wilt like the flower myself
A plant wilting from	my hair drooping, my skin
the hot sun.	getting drier and browner

As you can see, both of those lists have some "poetic" elements already. After we finished the observation sheet, we went back and looked for the words and phrases that we thought were strongest and combined them to create this short poem:

Summer Picnics

We sit on the deck
Browning in the sun
Like the smoke-toasted buns
That hug our grill-striped hot dogs.

Choosing the right words—words that are alive—helps make poetry vivid, too. Ted Hughes again:

Words that live are those which we hear, like "click" or "chuckle," or which we see, like "freckled" or "veined," or which we taste, like "vinegar" or "sugar," or touch, like "prickle" or "oily," or smell, like "tar" or "onion."°

The right word helps give you an image—a picture—of what you are describing and can also reproduce the rhythm, the movement of the thing.

°Ted Hughes, *Poetry Is*.

Comparisons also help create pictures for your reader. In "Bats" Randall Jarrell compares the bats' "high sharp cries" to "shining needlepoints of sound," and the image of sharpness comes to us clearly.° In "A Green Cornfield," Christina Rossetti compares a distant skylark to "a singing speck above the corn."† And in "Harvest Home," Herbert Read describes wagons at dusk as looking like "blue caravans."‡

Sometimes novice writers feel that a poem must rhyme. Of course, there are many poems that do rhyme, but much modern poetry does not. The important thing to remember when you are trying to write a poem is *not* to sacrifice your meaning to rhyme. Your poem should say exactly what you want it to. Mike Downey, a sportswriter for the *Detroit Free Press*, complains about the rhymed poems he receives about the Detroit Tigers:

> I appreciate the effort, but I wish people would stop sending me poems about the Tigers. Every one of them goes along the line of: "With Rozey and Lopey [two players] giving their all, the Tigers will be champions late in the fall." If you poetry writers have so much time, at least write me one that doesn't rhyme.°°

So, if you find you are having to create awkward sentences like this one:

> The black bird's eye did wink at me
> For my bag of crumbs I knew he could see

or if you're having to throw in language to make the lines the right length:

> The bubbling bath of the waterfall
> Made me want to give out a call

or if you're using trite or worn-out words to make a rhyme:

°Ted Hughes, *Poetry Is* (1970).
†Myra Cohn Livingston, *When You Are Alone* (1973).
‡Ted Hughes, *Poetry Is.*
°°Mike Downey, untitled column, *Detroit Free Press* (August 6, 1983).

95   Writing Fiction, Plays, and Poems

> As the ballerina danced
> I felt myself entranced

you will probably want to abandon the attempt to rhyme.

Most modern poets agree that poetry is increasingly like prose in its meter and rhyme. Often a sentence can be made into a poem just by rearranging it:

> Often
> a sentence
> can be made
> into
>   a poem
>   just
>   by
> rearranging it.

We don't mean to imply that poetry is the same as prose, or that you can become a poet by playing typing tricks as we did in the previous sentence. In general, poetry is more compressed and tight than prose, focusing on more restricted subjects, and dealing, as the poet Wordsworth said, "with powerful emotions recollected in tranquility."[*]

One of the best ways to sharpen your poetic skills is to read a great deal of poetry. As you read modern poetry, you'll come to see how it differs from prose, even though it may not rhyme. As you read older poems, you'll see how the writers of a different era used rhyme skillfully, without making it awkward or unconsciously humorous.

But the best way of all to learn to write poetry is to do it, letting the natural poetry of your soul and heart and experience flow onto the page. Byrd Baylor sums it up in a poem called "The Way to Start a Day." She

---

[*]William Wordsworth, preface to the *Lyrical Ballads* (1798).

suggests that the way to begin a new day is with song. Her advice applies to writing poetry as well:

> The way to make the song
> is this—
>
> Don't try to think
> what words to use
> until
> you're standing there
> alone.
> When you feel the sun
> you'll feel
> the song too.
>
> Just sing it.°

_____

°Byrd Baylor, "The Way to Start a Day," in *The Scribner Anthology for Young People.*

School Writing

7

Some readers may want to skip this chapter. Just a look at the chapter title may be enough to put them off. They may be reading this book because they're just plain sick of "school writing" and want to do more interesting writing on their own. They may even be the kind of writer described by Barbara Wersba, a young adult novelist:

> If you look at the lives of many writers, you see no . . . recognition in school . . . but the writer seems to be the person who keeps on writing.[*]

Such people may not want to be reminded of school writing and may be quite content to "keep on writing" on projects of their own.

There's another reason why some readers may want to skip the chapter: They're not old enough to have to worry much about writing in school or they're no longer in school. If that's the case, we'll simply suggest that you move on to Chapter Eight.

However, if you're in middle school or in junior or senior high school, you're probably doing more and more writing of reports and exams, and we'd advise you to "stay tuned" to this chapter. We'll provide you with some ideas and strategies for writing in school that draw on your outside interest in writing. We'll suggest some ways to turn dull and uninteresting

---

[*]Paul Janeczko, "An Interview with Barbara Wersba," *The English Journal* (November 1976).

school reports into writing that flexes your and your readers' imaginations, and we believe that's something even veterans of school writing—even those pulling down straight A's on their papers—will appreciate.

We won't offer you a "formula" or "model" for school reports and papers. Although you'll hear from time to time about models like "the five paragraph theme" (which introduces a topic in paragraph one, develops it in paragraphs two through four, and sums it up in paragraph five), we don't find such formulae especially helpful, and we know from teaching school ourselves that they often lead young writers to produce wooden, stilted, artificial writing structures.

We believe, with author Judith Guest, that "you become a good writer by writing. You just write and write." She adds:

> I was always intimidated by books that told you how to write. If I wasn't doing things exactly the way these books suggested, I thought, "Oh no, that means I don't have it. I can't do it." So I quit reading the books because I knew I wasn't going to quit writing.[°]

So we won't tell you how to write school papers. We believe that the more you write, whether poems, plays, letters, or school writing, the better you become at it. Moreover, one simple suggestion underlies everything we will write in this chapter:

Know your stuff.

Throughout this book we have stressed "writing from your own experience" and "writing about what you know." We suggested that's the key to good writing in general and to writing good letters, plays, poems, and stories. It is true for school writing as well. We know from our experience that when writers of all ages let the content and substance of writing be their guide, matters of form and structure often take care of themselves.

David Woodbury, a science writer, put it in a more sophisticated way when he said:

[°]Paul Janeczko, "An Interview with Judith Guest," *The English Journal* (March 1978).

An all-round knowledge of the subject is bound to shine through in your writing. It does more: it gives you confidence, and that comes through like a searchlight. °

When you are confident of what you are writing, when you have studied a topic to the point that you bubble over with ideas, it shows in your writing. You'll be better organized and write more clearly, with vigor and style, and maybe even a sense of humor (if you think your teacher will appreciate it). On the other hand, at times when you don't know your stuff, when your knowledge is shaky or you're just plain bored, that will show in your writing, too.

Now we're not going to give you a lecture or a pep talk, saying, "If you study hard, you'll write well and get good grades" (although there is some truth to that statement). Rather, we want to share with you a rather curious comment made by poet Jean Stafford about herself and other writers:

> Whether we are drowning Japanese beetles in turpentine, or gathering seashells by the seashore, or drinking up a storm at a cocktail party, we are at work as writers. We are eavesdropping and spying and asking questions and storing away the answers like pack rats. †

What does that have to do with school writing? Simply this: We suspect that as a writer you are more than ordinarily curious about things. You are an eavesdropper and listener and observer and rememberer. You are a *learner*, in short. If you can couple your learning skills with your knowledge of and interest in language, you will have a real advantage in doing school writing assignments.

° David Woodbury, "Writing About Science," in *Writers on Writing*, Herschell Brickell, ed. (1949) and reprinted in Floyd Watkins and Carl Knight, *Writer to Writer: Readings on the Craft of Writing* (1966).

† Jean Stafford, untitled article, *Saturday Review* (December 18, 1963).

Personal Notetaking

One place you can use your skills as a pack rat/observer/spy/listener is in notetaking, one of the most common kinds of school writing (so common many people don't think of it as *writing* at all). Sometimes notetaking will be as simple as copying an assignment or a word list. More often, however, and more interestingly, for certain, is notetaking that involves condensing a large amount of information. For example:

—You have read a chapter in your geography book in preparing for a test, so you condense all the basic information into a page of notes.

—You are assigned to give a speech in language arts, so you get your main ideas down on 3 x 5 inch cards.

—A guest speaker comes to class, and your teacher suggests that you take notes so you can ask good questions later.

In school, your teacher will, from time to time, ask you to present notes in outline form, using Roman numerals for main headings, capital letters for subheadings, Arabic numbers and lower case letters for further subheads. We always found in school that no matter how hard we tried, we couldn't get our notes into that form the first time, so we would write "rough draft notes" first, then put them in outline form later. Unfortunately, a lot of "real world" material doesn't follow outline form. The geography of Peru may only have two subheads, while the geography of Chile has fifteen; your speech for language arts has three main points, but no subheads at all; the guest speaker rambles, and you can't easily tell the major points from the minor.

We prefer to take notes by simply trying to keep a running record of the main points that come up, putting an asterisk (°) or dash (—) before each one. Just as it is with planning a piece of writing (see Chapter Four), a set of notes will often look confused and scratchy, with additions and subtractions and extra comments scrawled in the margins. When we are through, our notes look something like a road map in mountain country, with lines and squiggles twisting here and there.

By contrast, a well-organized friend of ours takes his notes in several different colors of ink, using bright red to identify major points, blue for lesser ideas and sub-points, then going back over the whole thing with a yellow felt-tip pen to highlight the especially important points. Frankly, we feel lucky if we can find *one* pen in pocket or purse when we need one, much less pens and markers in three colors, but our friend's use of color helps make an important point: Each person can develop a notetaking system to suit his or her personality.

You might like to take notes on 3 x 5 index cards, but you may find that cards get lost and scattered too easily and you prefer to use notebooks. If you are a notebook person, you may have a preference for three-ring loose-leaf binders, or you may like spiral-bound notebooks. Experiment with different possibilities and discover a system and style that work for you. Of course, if your teacher tells you to use a particular system for school work, by all means follow his or her rules. Save your experimenting for out-of-school projects.

Even more important than the notetaking system, however, is what you write down. Just as a writer is an active observer, you should concentrate on being an active notetaker, not just mechanically scribbling down someone else's ideas, but thinking, probing, questioning, learning—all the time using notes as a way of getting your ideas clear in your mind.

For instance, even before you start to take notes, you can be an active notetaker by writing down a few organizing questions for yourself. What are the important ideas you expect this textbook chapter to cover? What do you want to learn from this speaker? What questions do you have about the topic? How can this topic help you in your day-to-day living? These "pre-notetaking" notes will help you focus your attention, and when answers come up, whether in a lecture or a textbook chapter, you can recognize them and write them down.

Once you're into it—"it" being speech, textbook, or other information source—concentrate on being a *critical* notetaker. Some people have the idea that anything written in a book must be true, or that anything a well-known speaker says is right. However, most speakers and writers will admit that "the truth" and even "the facts" are often matters of impression, judgment, and interpretation. Individual biases and mistakes creep in. So as you read or listen and take notes, ask more questions: "How did she reach that conclusion?" "How did he get evidence for that?" "Does this really seem true?" "Do I accept what this person is telling me, or do I have doubts and ideas of my own?"

When you've completed your basic notes, spend a few minutes thinking and writing about what you've learned and observed. Write a *reaction* to the material. So what's the main idea? What have you learned? How does this strike you or impress you? How can you use this in your life? in school?

If you have been writing in a journal while reading this book, you'll recognize that this "reaction" phase is very much like what you do every day in your journal. In notetaking, however, you are reacting to someone else's ideas and experiences rather than your own. In doing so, you are using your notes to make that person's experience part of your own.

Summary, Precis, and Abstract

Unlike personal notetaking, in the *summary*, *precis* (pronounced PRAY-SEE), or *abstract*, you keep yourself and your opinions out of your writing. The assignment will be to condense all the ideas in a book or chapter or paper into a concise statement about a paragraph in length. Teachers will often assign a summary, precis, or abstract as a way of determining whether you've done your reading carefully. Even though you can't insert your opinion here, your personal notes provide you with a good start for writing. Look through your notes on a chapter or book, figure out the main or important points, then write your summary. Don't refer directly to the book when you are writing, since you may be inclined to borrow some of the author's language. Rather, write the summary and then reread or skim the original passage to make certain you've included all the important details.

To be honest, this kind of writing can be rather boring. To make a game of it, imagine that your real assignment is to serve as a record keeper for a dying planet. As Clerk #34567, your task is to help condense the knowledge of the planet's inhabitants into as few words as possible. You must be brief (all the reports will be stored on a single, finite microchip), and you must be accurate. If you play that game while writing your summary, precis, or abstract, you'll find your writing is very compact and solid.

Evaluations and Critiques

Unlike the summary, the *evaluation* or *critique* (pronounced CRIH-TEEK) *does* allow you to give your opinion, asking you to evaluate your reading or study, not just to summarize it. However, that doesn't mean that you can simply explode in anger or rant and rave, blasting something you don't like, or that you can bubble over with uncontrolled enthusiasm. For this kind of writing, sift through your personal notes, then summarize your reaction to what you've studied. Think not only about *what* you liked about it but *why*; tell not only *what* you disliked but *why*.

Perhaps the most common form of evaluation or critique that you write in school is the book report for language arts class. Your job there is, first, to let readers know what the book was about, and second, to let them know what you thought of it. It's not enough to tell a reader, "This is the greatest book ever written," or "I wouldn't read this book again in a million years if you paid me." Focus your likes and dislikes and explain why you responded as you did: "I liked it because the story kept me in suspense to the end." "I hated it because I knew from page one how it was going to end."

A good way to learn more about evaluations and critiques is to read samples of book, movie, and television reviews. You'll find these in most newspapers, especially the Saturday and Sunday editions. Study how professional writers summarize the book (or film or television program) without giving away the ending while mixing in their opinion about whether it was done well or badly.

When you are writing about books, you may enjoy writing something other than the usual "report." With your teacher's permission, consider one of the following alternatives:

—Imagine you are interviewing the author of the book. Make up questions and imaginary answers by the author. In the process of creating the answers, you'll be focusing your understanding of the book.

—Actually write a letter to the author, telling him or her what you liked and disliked about the book. Turn in a carbon copy of the letter to the teacher.

—Rewrite the ending of the book (or any other part of the book) and write an explanation of why you made those changes.

—Pretend you are in charge of turning the book into a movie or television program. What stars would you cast in the key roles? Where would the film be made? How would you "stage" or dramatize the book?

—Create a book jacket "blurb" for the book, a brief summary of its contents with a "come-on" enticing others to read it. (Read some book jackets at the library or bookstore to get models.)

Study Questions

Another kind of writing assignment you'll face more and more as you go through school is the *study question*, answering, in writing, the questions at the end of book chapters. These aren't always a lot of fun for a young writer, because such questions often call only for memory, not imagination, and for writing down someone else's ideas, not your own.

One way you can make your study questions more interesting, while practicing writing skills useful elsewhere, is to use them as a chance to think about audience or readers for your writing, and to practice putting yourself in the reader's shoes.

You've probably had the experience of reading something where an author seemed to forget about his or her readers. Perhaps the writer was explaining a complicated idea in science or math, or maybe just telling how to assemble a plastic model or a piece of hardware. Somewhere in the middle of the reading, you realized that you were lost, that you didn't understand what was happening. Yet the author was plowing merrily along writing about the Xanthophyl Theorem of Multiplication or telling you to "Fasten Bolt A to Nut B not neglecting to invert Flange C and to throttle Smorgasbord D before proceeding." The problem may have been yours, for you may simply have misread or read too quickly. Often, however, the author has lost you and has just plain failed to include enough information for you to follow along easily.

That can also happen to you as a writer when you answer study questions (or do things like giving instructions, writing directions, or explaining how to go about something). The idea is clear in *your* mind; you write it down; it *looks* clear to you. But something is left out, and the reader may not know whether the Ganges River is in India or South America or whether a hypotenuse is part of a triangle or a dread disease.

Putting yourself in the reader's shoes is no easy task, and professional writers struggle with it constantly. Practice through study questions by asking yourself:

—Did I define or explain all the *terms* that a reader needs to understand this?

—Could a stranger (not just your teacher) make sense of this?

—Is the sequence or order clear? Did I put first things first, second things second?

—Did I leave anything out? (Scan the chapter you are studying to remind yourself of what was covered.)

Also scan your answer for vague words, especially, "thing," "it," "its," and "it's." Whenever you see a "thing" or an "it," ask yourself whether it might be better to use the actual name: *bicycle pump, cactus, Pythagorean theorem.*

You can ask yourself the same set of questions when you do most school writing, whether essay or examination, and the answers will help you write more clearly for your audience.

Reports

When we talk with young writers in junior and senior high school (and even in elementary school), we find that the most common kind of school writing is something called "the report." A report can be anything from a one-page summary of an idea to a twenty- or thirty-page *term paper* or *research paper*, complete with *bibliography* (a list of books used in the research) and *footnotes* (notes explaining where material was found). You'll probably write dozens (and possibly hundreds) of reports during your school career.

The biggest complaint we hear from teachers about their students' reports, whether the long ones or the shorties, is that too often students just go to an encyclopedia, look up the topic, copy down the information (changing a few words), and turn it in. We'll guess that this "encyclopedia approach" sounds familiar to you and that you've done it from time to time—we certainly did when we were your age. Using the encyclopedia is no great evil, but the kind of information you find there is usually condensed, brief, and not terribly detailed. If you use the encyclopedia as your only source for a report, your writing tends to be flat and dull. As we recall it, copying out of an encyclopedia was pretty dull, too. There has to be a better way to go about it, beginning with how you pick your topic.

Choosing a Report Topic. Start by trying to make your report on a subject that genuinely interests you. Now, if your teacher tells you your report *must* be about Ukranian cheese exports in 1952, you're pretty much stuck (unless you're really excited about the topic of cheese exports). Generally, though, the teacher will give you a range of choices for your report, which allows you to draw on your interests and experiences. A professional or freelance writer will look for an "angle" on a story, which means approaching it from a unique or special point of view. You can do the same in writing reports.

For example, when we were working with a group of sixth and seventh graders, we gave them broad report topics centered on the four "elements" of science as perceived by the ancient Greeks: *Air*, *Earth*, *Water*, and *Fire*. We told them to find a special angle or interest area for these topics, and they were very imaginative in coming up with ideas. In studying *Air*, for instance, people wrote reports on everything from air pollution to rocketry (how a rocket moves through air) to hot air balloons and soaring. The writers about *Earth* covered problems from farming to travel to other planets. The students who picked *Water* did reports on topics as different as the diversion of water from the Great Lakes to the use of seaweed for food, and the *Fire* people wrote on everything from jet engine design to solar swimming pool heaters. In each case, the students took a broad topic and found ways to turn it into subjects that were interesting to them.

If you're absolutely stuck for a report topic, flip through the textbook for the class until something catches your eye: a fascinating photograph or chart, a curious statement, a fact that you just can't bring yourself to believe. Then ask yourself: "What can I make of this?" "How can I take this and turn it into a subject for a report?" "What's my *angle* on the topic?" In general, let your natural curiosity guide you in selecting a topic.

Above all, *don't* start writing on a topic that absolutely bores you to death. Talk to your teacher. Talk to other friends in the class. Even the dullest of studies has areas that will intrigue you or pique your interest.

Any topic that you select will probably be something you already know something about. (In fact, you'd be very unlikely to select a topic about which you were totally, abysmally, and utterly in the dark.) You probably could write a page or two of your report "off the top of your head," without looking for any further information. That would not be enough to sustain the report, but it helps you focus your study and research. In your journal or class notebook, write down what you already know about the subject, whether about comets and where they come from or the control of weeds in agriculture. Write freely and informally. If you're not sure of some of the facts, put question marks beside them.

Next, start thinking about what you *don't* know and what you want to find out. A good way to raise questions and think about where to go with your report is to create a "Question Web" as shown in Figure 7. Begin by writing your general report topic in the center of a sheet of paper. (We chose the topic of personal computers for this sample.) Then write down your questions as fast as you can. Often one question will lead to another, and pretty soon you will have a "web" or set of branches, each branch with related questions.

Through webbing you will probably raise even more questions than you can possibly answer in a single report, so you'll need to focus, discarding some of those questions or saving them for another report. Circle a branch of your web that contains the questions of greatest interest to you. (In our sample, we decided that the branch having to do with how silicon chips are made was most interesting, and we circled that with a dotted line.)

You can see, then, that before you rush off to the library and other places to do "research," using writing for planning can save you a lot of work and give focus to your study. For our computer report, for example, we've taken a very big topic, whittled it down to size, and selected a part of it for research that genuinely interests us.

Resources for Your Report. We asked a friend of ours who is a professional writer how he goes about researching his articles (or "reports").

"Do you go off to the library first?" we asked.

"The library?" he replied. "No. Libraries are great, and I do a lot of work there. But they're not the best place to begin."

"What's better?" we asked. "Where do you go?"

"To the people who know most about the subject," he answered. "I make a list of people who might be interviewed and go talk to them."

Our friend went on to explain that knowledgeable people can listen to his questions and pinpoint places to find answers. "They can even tell you what books to read."

Although you can't always find people to help you get started, we think our friend's advice is quite good. In doing the paper on silicon chips, for example, the best way to start studying might be by going to a local computer store to ask questions, rather than heading off to the library. Or we

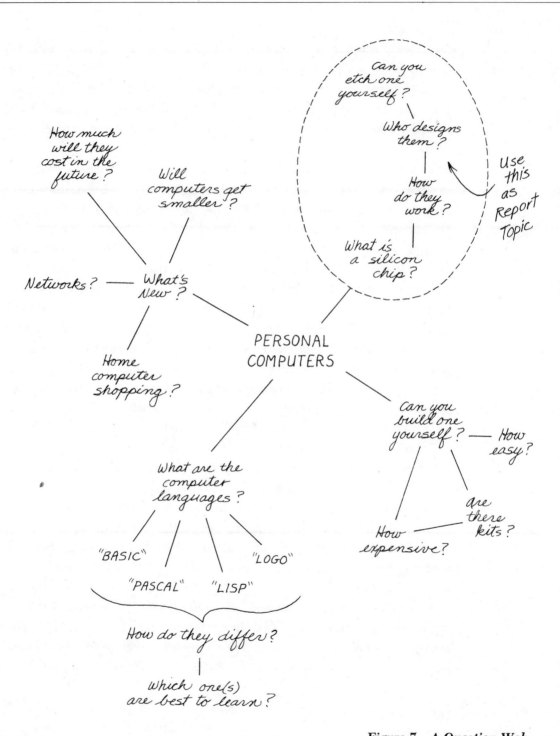

Figure 7   A Question Web

might try to make a contact at the computer science department of a university near us and ask a few questions.

Where you go and to whom you speak for your report will vary from one topic to another, but even if you live in a small town, there are people who can help you find answers to your questions. (We'll write more about this in the next chapter.) You'll find many experts on an amazing array of topics right around your school, and you'll find that you can interview fellow students, other teachers, school administrators, and staff on topics ranging from auto mechanics to computerized music. (We'll bet there's at least one student in practically every junior or senior high school in the country who could tell us how silicon chips are made.) You can also talk to your parents, neighbors, and community leaders about your topic.

(Note: Before you use people as a resource for writing your report, check it out with your teacher to make certain he or she approves. Some teachers don't want you to talk to outsiders about your report, and you must respect their wishes.)

When you've found the names of some people who might be able to help, shift your gears into "interviewer" and head out to meet them. Prepare for your interviews by listing some questions you want to ask; don't go to an interview planning to wing it by asking any question that pops into your mind. Take along a convenient notebook and scribble down answers. (Consider taking along a tape recorder and, with the person's permission, taping the interview so you can take notes at your leisure.) In any event, make certain you jot down the name of the person, the place of the interview, and the date. You'll need to include that information in your report.

The library might be a good next stop on your quest for information. We won't say much about the library, because we assume you already know how to use one. Suffice it to say, if you read an encyclopedia article about your topic, *don't stop there.* Use all the resources that you are likely to find in a school or town library: nonfiction books, magazines, files (collections of clippings on particular topics), newspapers (sometimes available on microfilm or microfiche), and even films, slides, and recordings. If you're having trouble figuring out where to look, ask the librarian for help. As you look up library materials, keep notes on your sources. These will be helpful in compiling a bibliography for your report (see Figure 8).

You may even want to do some original experimentation and research for your report. In addition to using people and books for information, you can discover answers to questions yourself.

For example, you might develop a *questionnaire* to be administered to fellow students or people around town about your topic. This would ask a few questions about what people think, feel, and know about a topic. As part of our silicon chip report, for example, it might be interesting to find out how many people know (or think they know) what a chip is or whether they know that chips are the heart of a computer.

Some reports may also lead you to conduct simple experiments to find answers. In the writing project we described earlier, our students grew seeds under controlled conditions to answer questions about *Earth*, shot rockets into the air to experiment with *Fire* and *Air*, and cooked seaweed foods and asked friends to evaluate the taste while discovering things about *Water*. Original experiments add real class and originality to a report, lifting it a notch above reports routinely done in the library.

You can see that, on the whole, there are many alternative resources to use in preparing a report. In a given report, you won't use all these resources, but you should probably use several—at least if you want to go about writing as a real writer would.

Writing the Report. Let's say you've accumulated pages and pages of notes and information on your topic. While other kids content themselves with copying the facts out of encyclopedias, you can be at work sifting through your information. Do some journal writing at this point, answering some of these questions:

—What did I learn that's new?

—What did I learn that's exciting?

—What seem to be the most important issues or problems associated with my topic?

Figure 8 *Preparing a Bibliography*

A bibliography is simply a list of books (and other materials) referred to in a report. The bibliography usually appears at the end of a report, alphabetized, with the author's last name first. We think it works best to keep bibliography notes on individual index cards, which makes the alphabetizing easier. You can also use a bibliography at the early stages of your report as a way of deciding what you want to read or examine.

Your teacher may have a specific form or pattern for you to follow in preparing your "bib," and you should always follow the teacher's instructions. However, here is a general pattern for bibliographies that we find helpful. Note that the *punctuation marks* and the *use of capitals* is an important part of bibliography form. You should use the same pattern throughout.

A bibliography item can/should include:

Author's name.	Last name first, followed by a comma, first name, period.
Title of magazine article or chapter.	Enclose this in quotation marks, follow by a comma.
Title of book.	Underline, follow by a period.
Publication information.	City of publication, colon, publisher, comma, date. For magazines, put date in parentheses.

FOR EXAMPLE:

Book
> Uris, Leon. *Topaz.* New York: Bantam Books, 1963.

Magazine Article.
> Willis, Jamie. "Out West and Down Home," *Country Music Journal* (April 1978).

You can also add page numbers if you think that would be helpful to a reader. The important thing about a bibliography is that it shows a reader precisely where you got your information; it "documents" your statements and assertions.

—What's the most important "news" I have to share with my teacher and classmates?

Historian Peter Gay observes; "Facts are never neutral; they are impregnated by value judgments."* By that he implies that writers move from collecting facts to interpreting them and explaining them for an audience. By answering the questions above and by writing in your journal, you will be moving toward establishing your own, fresh point of view on the topic.

You might also want to consider alternative forms of writing up your report. Instead of simply doing a report in which you list and discuss a lot of facts and information, consider doing your report as:

—a dialog between yourself and a make-believe expert in the field.

—a script for a radio program.

—a short story based on your knowledge (for example, a short story about how one computer company steals computer chip designs from another).

—a series of poems.

Think of ways of using your unique resources as well. If you tape recorded interviews, for example, you might want to play some of those interviews as part of an oral report. If you collected some interesting posters or brochures on the topic, do a bulletin board or poster display, with written captions. A report can be done on film (a photo essay), as a drama (perhaps performed for the school's video cameras), or even as a debate (with debaters "primed" by you, the expert).

We haven't, in this section, said anything about how to organize or actually write the report. That has been covered in Chapter Four. Because report topics differ so much, and because the content of a report will vary so widely, there are no fixed rules to follow, except the one we offered for this chapter:

Know your stuff.

If you have a firm grasp on your information, if you've collected information from several sources (see Figure 9), and if you've tried to focus your ideas for an audience, you'll find that the writing will go smoothly.

---

*Peter Gay, *Style in History* (1976).

Figure 9 *Footnotes*

Many teachers will ask you to include footnotes with your report. In general, if you are quoting another person or referring directly to a book or magazine article, you should write a footnote. Put a number in your text at the end of the quote or reference. Then at the bottom of the page (or at the end of the report), write the footnote. The pattern for a footnote is only slightly different from that of a bibliography. Though your teacher may specify a form, this general plan will work for most footnotes. Be certain to follow the pattern for punctuation marks, underlining, quotes, and capitals.

Footnote number Author's name—first followed by last, "Title of Magazine Article or Book Chapter," *Title of Book* (City of Publication: Publisher, Date or Date of Magazine), page numbers.

FOR EXAMPLE:

[1]Leon Uris, *Topaz* (New York: Bantam Books, 1963), p. 46.
[2]Jamie Willis, "Out West and Down Home," *Country Music Journal* (April 1978), p. 13.

Examinations

The single most difficult and anxiety-producing school writing is the examination. Usually in an exam a teacher asks you a question and gives you a limited amount of time to answer. Painful as exams are, you might as well learn to write them well, since you'll be writing them for years to come.

Once again, we have to offer the advice:

Know your stuff.

If you've studied hard and learned the material, the actual writing of the exam will be as easy as exam writing ever is. There are other pointers we've picked up, both from writing examinations ourselves and from interviewing young people who have taken exams:

1. *Read the question carefully.* Make certain you understand what's being asked for. Reread the question twice or even three times before moving on.

2. *Take time to organize.* Even if it's only for three or four minutes, it will pay you to jot down some ideas on scratch paper about how you want to handle the question.

3. *Write with your reader in mind.* Your teacher will be reading thirty or more similar papers and will be looking for answers to specific questions. Keep your teacher in mind and concentrate on showing him or her that you do, in fact, know your stuff.

4. *Be lively and imaginative in your writing.* You are a *writer*, after all, not just a scribbler or a copyist. Unlike many of your classmates, you enjoy writing and playing with language. Without being smarty or cutesy, let your personality and your writing style show through. In other words, *write naturally*. Don't start using extra-long sentences or highfalutin' words thinking you'll impress the teacher.

5. *Leave time for proofreading.* Even if it's only for three to five minutes, make certain you proofread carefully. In exams, you often write in haste as you go along. A brief proofreading session to check over spelling, mechanics, grammar, and so on will add points in the teacher's grade book. (More on proofreading in Chapter Nine.)

Write Around Town

8

Your hometown is a gold mine of writing opportunities. Whether you live in a city of a million people or a small town of just a few hundred people, you'll find that by visiting THE BUTCHER, THE BAKER, or THE CANDLESTICK MAKER you can find interesting topics to explore in writing.

Do you doubt us? Let's take the three merchants mentioned in the previous paragraph and consider how their shops might lead to writing ideas.

THE BUTCHER SHOP—Nowadays there aren't very many true "butcher shops," stores that specialize in selling fresh meat exclusively. (Writing ideas! What happened to the olde tyme butcher shops? What were they like?) The modern butcher shop is likely to be the meat department in a supermarket, but if you go there, you'll find some butchers who can tell you about their work. What kinds of stories could you write? Consider:

—a story about how butchers are trained for and learn their craft.

—a description with diagrams of different cuts of meat and how they are prepared and priced. (Why is steak so much more expensive than hamburger? What *is* hamburger, anyway?)

—an essay describing how butchers wrap and label those see-through packages you buy at the store.

THE BAKER—Here you might visit a local bakery, a doughnut shop, or even a huge commercial bakery that turns out loaves of bread by the thousands. Depending on which baker you visit, you could write an interesting paper on:

117

—the hours bakers work. (What time does the doughnut shop owner get up to go to work?)

—how yeast makes things rise.

—the different kinds and varieties of doughnuts.

—what happens to the hole part of the doughnut.

THE CANDLESTICK MAKER—Here we're stretching the point a bit, because if you look in the phone book, you probably won't actually find a candlestick maker listed. However, if you visit a woodworking shop, you can probably find someone who will show you how wooden candlesticks are turned on a lathe. If there's a knitting mill nearby, you might learn that discarded spools for thread and yarn are often recycled and sold as candlesticks. And if you go to a jewelry store, you might look at some very expensive candlesticks and write about what they're made of and where they come from.

Feature and Local Color Articles

Got the idea? To find story ideas, all you have to do is cultivate your curiosity and "write around town."

Most of the stories you write from this chapter will fall into the professional writing category of the "feature article" or the "local color piece." These are the sorts of stories that generally appear after page three—after the "hard" news—in a newspaper or in the Sunday supplement. These are stories about interesting people, places, and things. In magazines, you'll find feature articles about places to visit, things to buy, ideas to try in your own home. If you study feature articles in print, you'll see that professional writers have trained themselves to see the writing possibilities in places where they live and visit. They often take ordinary or commonplace information about their town and spin it into stories and articles that amuse and entertain.

Some of the "write around town" stories you write will be "how to" pieces in which you share something you've learned: how to tie fishing flies, how to make pizza. Other stories may simply provide information or little known facts: how an electrical air purifier works, how cable television signals get to your home. Some stories may be based on interviews: with a banker who has worked in your town for forty years, with a man who restores antique clocks. Some pieces may be about colorful local spots: a neighborhood "cigar store," a special rose garden in a city park.

As you see feature articles in your regular reading, think about them from the point of view of the writer. How was this story developed? Where did the author go? Whom did she visit? Where did the information come from? Was any library work involved? That way you'll sharpen your own sense of how to go about developing your own stories.

The A to Z of Writing Around Town

Later in this chapter we'll discuss some techniques and strategies for researching and writing your story. First, though, we want to show you the full potential of writing in your town by giving examples of projects and article ideas from A to Z. Almost every one of these places will be found in small or large towns. For each, we'll suggest some questions which we think could lead a young (or experienced) writer to a good idea for a story.

AIRPORT—How do you get a pilot's license? What's the difference between small and large airports? Who owns the airport? Who manages it? Where do planes fly?

BEEKEEPER—(Yes, there probably is one in your town, though you may have to ask around to find him or her.) Is it dangerous to keep bees? What equipment do you use? How do you get the bees? How do you keep from bee-ing stung? What does a beekeeper sell? Is beekeeping fun? Is it a business or hobby?

COLLECTORS' SHOPS—Study the objects people collect, from baseball cards to beer cans. What determines whether an object is valuable? What are the "rules" of collecting? How does one start a collection? How does one sell valuable objects? Are there counterfeit collectibles?

DETECTIVE AGENCY—How does a real detective agency differ from the kind you see on TV? What do the agencies detect? How expensive are they? How do people train to become detectives?

ELECTRIC POWER COMPANY—Where does the electricity in your town come from? How is it generated? Does any of it come from nuclear plants? from coal plants? from hydroelectric (water driven) plants? What kind of equipment does the power company use to control the flow of "juice"? How does the power company make plans to cope with emergencies?

FLORIST—Does the florist grow his/her own flowers? Where do other plants come from? What kinds of flowers do people most like to buy? How can you keep houseplants healthy? How does one send flowers "by telegraph"?

GAS STATION—Where does the gasoline we use come from? How does it get from the ground to your town? Why have gas prices gone up so much in recent years? What services do different kinds of local gas stations offer? Which ones give you free air for your bicycle tires?

HARDWARE STORE—(You think of the possibilities here. Just go to a good hardware store and browse around looking at things. You'll come up with dozens of things to write about.)

ICE CREAM SHOP—How many flavors are available, how often do they change, and who decides what flavors will be offered? What are the most popular flavors? Do people mostly want cones or sundaes or other things? (Think of the possibilities of interviewing customers here.)

JUKEBOX DISTRIBUTOR—How much is a jukebox worth? Who picks the songs? How much money does a jukebox take in on a good day or week?

KEY MAKER—How many different kinds of keys and locks are sold? How do locks and keys work? How do combination locks work? Can you really crack a safe as they do on TV? How can you get yourself into your house or car if you've locked yourself out? What is a skeleton key?

LABORATORIES: MEDICAL, DENTAL, OR SCIENTIFIC—What

labs operate in your town? What do they do? Visit a lab and ask questions about its operations and purposes. What kinds of writing do lab technicians and administrators have to do?

MUSEUMS: ART, HISTORICAL, SCIENTIFIC—(Just visit the museum with notebook in hand and write down the questions that occur to you. You could write for *years* on the topics you'll discover in a museum, even a small one.)

NEWSPAPER—How is the news written? How many people write for the paper? Is there any way a person your age can write for or work for the paper? How is the newspaper printed and distributed? How are various kinds of stories written: sports, family living, reviews? What are the best journalism schools?

OFFICE SUPPLY STORE—(Visit the store and ask questions based on the supplies and equipment you see there.) What is all this stuff for? Who uses it? What's new in office furniture and equipment?

PANCAKE HOUSE—How many flavors of pancakes do they make? How do you cook a truly perfect pancake?

QUICK PRINTER—What printing processes does the printer use? How does he/she set type and prepare "camera ready" copy? How has printing changed since Gutenberg's day? How is it likely to change in the future? How does one print in multiple colors? How are booklets made, assembled, and bound? (As a writer, you'll be especially interested in this place, since you'll learn how words are produced in print. Ask the printer if he/she knows of people engaged in "self-publishing": putting out their own writing without the benefit of a regular publisher. Interview them.)

RADIO STATION—How does the transmitter work? What does it transmit? Who decides what goes on the air? What logs and records does the radio station maintain? How do the folks in charge know who's listening? How far away can local stations be heard? What public service features does the station produce or air?

SALVAGE STORE—What do salvage operations salvage? Why? What do they do with what they've salvaged? Who shops at a salvage store?

TAXIDERMIST—Where does the taxidermist learn his/her trade? Where do the animals to be stuffed come from? How does the taxidermist get the insides out and the stuffing back in?

UPHOLSTERY SHOP—How does the upholsterer turn a ratty-looking couch or chair into a beautiful "new" one?

VACUUM CLEANER STORE—How do vacuum cleaners work? What are the best brands? Why do vacuum cleaners break down? How can they be repaired?

WASTE REMOVAL SERVICE—Where does all the garbage go?

X-RAY LABORATORY—What sorts of X rays does the lab take? How does X-ray equipment work? Is it safe? What health and safety precautions do the technicians follow? How do you get to be an X-ray technician?

YACHT CLUB—How big, fast, and expensive are boats that people buy for recreational purposes? Where do people use their boats? (Note: If you're in bone-dry territory, substitute a visit to a place that sells OFF-THE-ROAD VEHICLES and ask the same questions.)

ZIPPER REPAIR SHOP—(We admit we were stretching to find a place beginning with Z. Check your phone book looking for Z places. We found that zipper repairs are done by a TAILOR or at a FIXIT SHOP.) How do zippers work? Who invented the zipper? What modern materials are used in zipper construction? Will zippers ever be replaced by other kinds of fastenings?

Well, there you have the A to Z of writing around town. We suspect that even as you read that list, you started thinking of places you'd like to visit in your town, of agencies and shops and institutions that could yield interesting stories.

Researching and Writing the Story

Visiting Places and People. The write-around-town story involves face-to-face or face-to-place contact: You'll need to go places, notebook (and possibly camera and/or tape recorder) in hand, to collect information, to do your research. Here are a few guidelines you should follow to ensure that your data collecting goes smoothly:

1. *Make an appointment before you visit.* You can telephone or send a letter. Explain that you are a (young) writer doing a story; could you come and talk to someone? A few places will not want to be bothered and will tell you so, but most places around town will welcome you, and often they'll make special efforts to ensure that you are greeted and shown around.

2. *Make a list of the questions you want to ask.* This will help you get started in an organized fashion. Once you're there, additional questions will occur to you.

3. *Be on time for your appointment.*

4. *Take quick notes on the scene.* You won't have time to write long descriptions, but carry a small pad and jot down key words and phrases to help you in writing up ideas later. (See item 8.)

5. *Collect handouts.* Most places you visit will have fliers, leaflets, mimeographed sheets, or advertising brochures telling you about their business or profession. Save as many of these as you can for reference later.

6. *Carry a camera and take a few pictures.* Ask permission.

7. *Carry a tape recorder and record interviews.* Again, ask permission, since some people will not want to be recorded. (You might also tape record some of the *noises* of the place to remind yourself later what it was like.)

8. *Write longer notes right after your visit.* Sit on a park bench outside the place or at a nearby fast food restaurant and "debrief" yourself in your journal, recapturing as much of your visit as you can.

Planning and Writing. Often your story will pretty much "write itself," since the interesting information and ideas will stand out in your mind. Nevertheless, here are some pointers that may make the job go more smoothly:

1. *Think about an audience for your story.* Many of your feature articles can actually be used as school reports, in which case your audience will be your teacher and your classmates. However, you may also be able to publish your piece in the school paper or literary magazine, in which case you'll be writing for all the students, plus the faculty, staff, and even parents. It

may be that your local newspaper will consider stories written by someone your age; in that case, you'll be writing for an audience of community members ranging in age from eight to eighty. Or you may, in your visit to a local factory or store, find that the owner (or his/her public relations assistant) would like to print your story as part of an "in house" newspaper or newsletter for employees; if so, you'll be writing for people who already know the business, but are interested in fresh ideas and perceptions of it.

2. *Slant your story to your audience.* Ask yourself, "What will this group of readers be most interested in knowing about? Or even better, interview a few people in that potential audience, telling them your general topic and asking what they would most like to know. You don't have to write exactly what they want to hear, but your writing will be more focused if you've thought about your readers, not just your own interests.

3. *List the main ideas or points of the story; then rank them in importance.* That listing will give you a "plot" or outline to follow in writing.

4. *Start with an example or illustration.* Don't begin this article (as you might begin a school essay) by saying, "In this report I'm going to tell you about . . ." Instead, plunge into your story with an example or description: a nice quote from someone you interviewed; a description of the place, done in your most vivid language; a description of an incident or operation you saw during your visit.

5. *Let your research carry the story.* Your knowledge of the place and the people who work there will create the "stuff" of your writing; all you have to do is make certain you have described them clearly.

6. *Have someone from your audience read your rough draft.* Once you've gotten your ideas on paper, even in fairly rough form, get some reader response. Is what you've written clear? Does it answer the reader's questions? Does it speak to the interests of the reader? What parts were more interesting than others to your potential audience?

7. *Prepare a graphic display to go with your story.* Most, but not all, feature articles have pictures and illustrations to go with them. If you've taken photographs, select the best, write captions, and include them with

your story. If you collected handouts, consider including part of a company brochure or flier with your story as an illustration. Draw a chart or sketch of a complex machine. Make a map of the floor layout of an assembly line. All these graphic materials will help enhance your story, and if you actually get it published, your editor may well want to use them, too.

WRITE AROUND TOWN!

How to Be Your Own Editor

9

We'll begin this chapter by quoting a piece of advice you've probably heard a dozen times, perhaps from teachers or from professional writers:

There is no good writing, only good rewriting.

This suggests that after you've completed a draft of your work, the job is only partly done. We think it is extreme to suggest that it's *impossible* to do good writing on a first draft, or that if you don't rewrite your work will be bad. However, the experience of most writers and teachers is that if you want to write your best, you must be concerned with revising as well as writing.

Alexander Pope, the eighteenth-century British poet, phrased it this way:

True ease in writing comes from
art, not chance.[*]

He meant that prose (or poetry) that looks smooth or flowing is often the result of careful and laborious revising.

What do we mean by revising? That may seem like an obvious question, but we've found that many novice writers have only a foggy idea of what it means. To some, "revising" means merely copying a composition over on good clean paper and in their best handwriting, something they may

---

[*]Alexander Pope, "Essay on Criticism" (1711).

126

have learned from teachers who placed a premium on penmanship. Of course, preparing neat final copy is an important end to the writing process, but it is not the heart of revising. Other young writers equate revising with getting a paper into "good English," checking it over for errors in spelling, punctuation, and grammar. Correctness, too, is important in writing, and toward the end of the process of preparing a piece of writing, the author must carefully check it for errors in language, but again, that is not the essence of revising.

To us, revising means working with the *content, structure,* and *style* of your writing until it says what you want to say just the way you want it said. Revising a paper sometimes means throwing away several pages and doing them over because they weren't coming out right. It may mean shifting around the parts of an essay to create a clearer, better organized piece. It can mean "fine tuning" your language to get just the right word to express your ideas.

Jonathan Swift, the British poet and satirist, summed up the essential steps in revising this way:

Blot out, correct, insert, refine.
Enlarge, diminish, interline.°

When you revise, you will often "blot out," erasing or scratching out what you see as bad writing or unneccessary words; you will "correct" errors (mistakes in both content and grammar); you will "insert" new information or substitute words, sometimes "interlining" (writing between the lines of your draft); you will "refine" your language and make it more precise; you may "enlarge," expanding sections that seem to need more attention; you may "diminish," reducing the relative emphasis of some parts of a piece. (A sample of one of our revised pages—blotted, interlined, thoroughly revised—is shown in Figure 10.)

°Jonathan Swift, "On Poetry" (1733).

Chapter Nine:

HOW TO BE YOUR OWN EDITOR

We'll begin this chapter by quoting a piece
of advice you've probably heard a dozen times,
perhaps form teachers or professional writers:

There is no good writing,

only good rewriting.

This ~~advice~~ suggests that after you've completed a
draft of your work, ~~getting your ideas down on~~
~~paper~~, the job is only partly done. We think it
may be extreme to suggest that it's impossible to
do "good" writing on a first draft, or that if you
don't rewriter, your work will be bad. However, ~~but~~ the
experience of most writers and teachers is that if
you want to writer your best, you must be
concerned with revising as well as writing.

Alexander Pope, the eighteenth tenth century
British poet, phrased it this
way:

"True ease in writing
comes from art, not chance."

Figure 10

Revising may take quite a bit of time, and many writers are almost compulsive about making changes in their work. Ernest Hemingway said he wrote and rewrote the ending to *A Farewell to Arms* over forty times, adding (reminiscent of Alexander Pope), "but I hope it doesn't read that way."* Novelist John Gunther reported that he liked to "fiddle and faddle" with a manuscript, sometimes making changes while in a cab delivering his "final" manuscript to an editor.† Paul Zindel claims to have trouble "letting go" of a manuscript, because he always wants to make just one more change, one last adjustment, before turning it over to a publisher.‡ Good writers are tinkerers with their writing.

Often writers have help with revision from editors, and it may be that you'll have a chance to work with an editor, perhaps the editor of a school paper or literary magazine, or the editor of a magazine that has agreed to publish something you've written. Your teacher will often serve as your editor for school writing, offering advice and suggestions for needed revisions. Your editor may raise questions about what you wrote (or meant to write); she may ask for additional writing or information ("enlarging"); he may suggest that whole sections will have to be cut ("diminishing").

We have a suggestion to offer you in reacting to your editor:

Don't argue!

Sometimes what an editor says will make you angry, and editors are often quite blunt and direct in their criticism. You may want to fight back and say, "But you didn't understand!" or, "You read it all wrong!" Editors do make mistakes, of course, but it doesn't do much good to argue. A better practice for the writer, we think, is this: Pay close attention to your editor's advice, but remember that *you* are the author. In the end, your editor (or teacher) will count on you to make good revisions based on your best ideas and thoughts. It's *your* manuscript, not his or hers. Remembering that your

---

*Ernest Hemingway, "Letter to Charles Poore," in *Ernest Hemingway, Selected Letters*, Carlos Baker, ed. (1981).

†Floyd Watkins and Carl Knight, *Writer to Writer: Readings on the Craft of Writing* (1965).

‡Paul Janeczko, "An Interview with Paul Zindel," *The English Journal* (October 1977).

editor has a pretty good idea of what people like to read, and that he/she has worked with a lot of writing, use your editor's advice and suggestions while remaining your own boss.

Another reason for remaining your own boss is that often you simply won't have an editor to help you. (As a matter of fact, even professional authors don't get editorial help until they've done several revisions on their own.) We think it important, then, for you to learn how to be your own editor, learning to make changes and improvements in your work based on your developing sense of what's good and bad writing. Robert Graves and Richard Hodge have suggested that you must learn to be "the reader over your shoulder":

> We suggest that whenever anyone sits down to write, he should imagine a crowd of prospective readers . . . looking over his shoulder. They will be asking such questions as: "What does this sentence mean?" "Why have you chosen such a ridiculous metaphor?" "Must I really read this long, limping sentence?" "Haven't you got your ideas muddled here?"*

Art Spikol, a freelance writer and publisher, suggests:

> Excellent writers are . . . usually good editors. They're the ones that do what an editor would otherwise have to do—but they do it first.†

In the remainder of this chapter, we'll suggest some strategies for you to use in revising your own work. Then we'll go on to discuss some of those other aspects of writing—*proofreading* and *copy preparation*—that are also important (but not as important as revising).

---

*Robert Graves and Richard Hodge, *The Reader Over Your Shoulder* (1943).
†Art Spikol, "Self-Editing," *Writer's Digest* (January 1983).

How to Edit a Paper

When you've just finished drafting a paper, it may be tempting to turn right around and begin editing it. However, if you do, you'll often miss items that you really should change. Why? For one thing, your writing often looks extraordinarily good to you just after you've completed it. Hard work went into it, and you feel satisfied, rewarded. "It's mine! It's beautiful! It's *done*! Don't change a comma!" For another, when you have finished drafting, you remember too clearly just what you "meant" to say. You read that fresh draft as if it says exactly what you wanted it to say. Thus you read "new" writing with a kind of blindness, missing some problems that other readers will encounter.

Letting Writing Cool. A partial solution to that blindness is to let your writing "cool down" before you try to do anything with it. Put your writing away for a day or two before you begin revising. (Of course, in many school assignments, that won't be possible, because the assignment is due the next day.) After some time has passed, resume work and you'll find that you can approach your writing with "open eyes." You'll have forgotten what it was you meant in that curious sentence in paragraph two. And the joke in paragraph four that seemed so funny at the time now just looks corny. You'll be able to think of different ways of saying things that will make your meaning even clearer to the reader. In short, you'll no longer be so close to the writing that you can't see its weaknesses.

Reading Aloud. Start the revising process by reading your work aloud to yourself. At first that may seem silly, or it may make you self-conscious, but give it a try. If you're embarrassed, lock yourself in your room and turn up a radio or record player so nobody else can hear you. (In school you can "read aloud silently" to yourself, moving your lips but not pronouncing the words aloud.) This oral reading forces you to read *word by word*, not skipping any. It also gives you a feeling for how the work sounds. You'll instantly discover some mistakes in your writing as you read aloud, some that you would skip over or forgive yourself for if you were doing a silent reading. The oral reading allows you to answer some important questions about your paper:

—Does this *sound* like me? Is this my natural writing/speaking voice? (Or does the writing sound as if I'm trying to be someone else?)

—Does the content flow from one idea to the next?

—Are there any clunky phrases and words that catch the ear unpleasantly?

A Friendly Reading. If possible, have a friend read your paper next to make suggestions. (If you're writing for school, check with your teacher first to make certain that kind of assistance is allowed.) Your friend can be a parent, neighbor, your boyfriend or girlfriend, or a just plain friend. It's important, though, to get someone who will be honest with you in reacting to your work—someone who will tell you directly what his/her reaction is.

You may want to read your paper aloud to the friend, especially if your rough draft handwriting is bad, but many writers prefer to have the friend read the paper silently from their manuscript. That way the reader is forced to come up with meanings on his/her own, not catching any clues from the tone of the writer's voice.

When the reading is finished, ask for reactions. Don't just say, "What didja think?" or "How didja like it?" Those questions are too broad and invite your reader to give you rather vague answers like, "Well, it was okay!" or "Gee, I don't know." Ask your reader to be specific in replying to such questions as:

—Can you summarize it? Tell me the main ideas.

—What specific parts of the writing caught your eye or attracted your interest?

—What are its greatest strengths?

—What should I work on next?

As we said when we were discussing editors, it's important for you not to argue with your readers. There will be times when your friend won't especially like what you've written. Don't get in a snit and dismiss that person as a friend. Realize that *your writing* created the impression in the reader's mind, whether that impression is right or wrong, favorable or unfavorable. If you think your friend totally misunderstood your writing, ask yourself, "What went wrong?"

Multiple Readers. Because reader reactions differ, you might want to get several readings from friends at this point. If you think one friend misread your paper, try another. If the same "misreading" occurs, then you know you've got trouble. With several readers, too, you'll be able to form a *consensus* in your mind, summarizing different opinions to get a main direction for revision of your work.

Analyzing Strengths and Weaknesses. Whether or not you've taken our advice about getting outside readers and reading your paper aloud, at this point, get out a sheet of paper and make two columns:

Strengths   Weaknesses

List what you see as the strong points of your draft; then list the parts that are weak or not to your satisfaction. Then in the center of the page write:

Aims for Revision

In order of importance, write down what you want to change. Maybe your opening is high priority: It just doesn't engage the reader. Perhaps you feel you need more development to your argument in the middle. Maybe the whole thing sounds too weighty and ponderous and needs some lightening up. Don't feel that this list must be terribly long or exhaustive. If you can get down one or two good solid goals for revising, you'll be moving toward an excellent revision.

Revising for Specifics. Well, that's about enough preparation for revising. Having thought about the paper, read it aloud, and blocked out some goals for yourself, you can now pick up a pen or pencil and start "hackin' and hewin'" at your text, marking the changes you think are appropriate. You can "interline," add inserts on the backs of pages, even take a scissors to your work, cutting out sections that are to be discarded or moved elsewhere (there to be taped into place). You may want to learn how to use a standard set of proofreader's symbols, which are simply a code for indicating changes on a manuscript. Some of these symbols are shown in Diane

Rodgers's poem (Figure 11). Also check any dictionary or writer's guide to learn the complete proofreader's code.

You may find it helpful to think about revisions to your paper in three categories:

1. *Content and Organization*. This is the "big one," both in the sense of requiring big changes and in being very important to the success of your paper. Look at the overall plan or pattern of your paper. Does it say what you want it to say? (Could your readers summarize the main ideas easily?) Is it long enough? Too long? Have you included enough information? Too much? Can you move parts around for greater clarity? Does it have an engaging opening? A firm and solid conclusion?

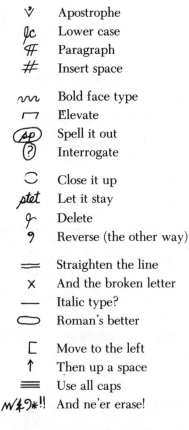

ᵛ	Apostrophe
lc	Lower case
⁋	Paragraph
#	Insert space
∿	Bold face type
⌐	Elevate
(ⓢⓟ)	Spell it out
(?)	Interrogate
◡	Close it up
stet	Let it stay
ℊ	Delete
⁹	Reverse (the other way)
=	Straighten the line
×	And the broken letter
—	Italic type?
�	Roman's better
[	Move to the left
↑	Then up a space
≡	Use all caps
⩘⁹✱‼	And ne'er erase!

Figure 11 *Proofreader's Plea*

2. *Audience*. Think about those readers again, including your friends who responded to your draft. Are you writing *for* them and *to* them? Are you thinking about their interests? It might be useful for you to pause in your revising for a few minutes and try to conjure up in your mind a picture of your readers. Just who are these folks? What do they like to read? Imagine yourself standing in front of them telling them orally about your writing. What parts would you emphasize to them? Are those the parts that stand out most in your writing?

3. *Language and Style*. The most difficult kind of revising takes place in this category, because it is difficult to know whether your language and style are "right." By "language," we mean that the language you choose creates a certain tone or style for your paper. Look back in this chapter to the quote by Graves and Hodge. Could you tell from the passage that they are British? What are the clues? We find that some of their phrases like "Must I really read this long, limping sentence?" or "Haven't you got your ideas muddled here?" have a formal sound and tone we associate with British English. By contrast, Art Spikol's statement, immediately following, seems folksy, casual, and "American" because of his use of contractions like "they're" and the tacked on "but they do it first."

One can't predictably tell national origin based on language style, but the differences between those two passages help us point out what we mean by style and language. Your choices of words, phrases, and sentences help to create the tone of your work. You can, at times, be formal, informal, folksy, stuffy, erudite (learned), haughty, or tough. Read your writing; figure out what tone it achieves (with the help of your friendly readers); decide if that's the tone you want; change words and phrases if you need to.

A very good test of style for the beginning or young writer is to ask: Do I use this kind of language every day? While you shouldn't write exactly the way you talk, your day-to-day conversation can be a good guide to the tone of your writing. If you are writing naturally, the answer to that question will be "yes." When you're older and more experienced, you can experiment with your style, moving away from conversational words and phrases to achieve different effects.

Finishing Touches on Revision. You'll find that revising a paper may take as much or more time than the original writing. (Remember that good writing is "art, not chance.") Don't overdo your revising, of course, or spend so much time on a paper that you get sick of the writing or drain the life out of it. When you think you've gotten your work to the point you want, then give it the final acid test: Read it aloud to yourself *again*. You'll know by the time you've finished whether you've gotten the content, structure, language, and style the way you want them.

(Note: Before moving on to the next stage, you might need to make a clean copy of your work. This needn't be letter perfect, but at least recopy the parts that have gotten quite messy. Make certain you can read everything easily.)

Achieving Correctness in Writing

The next stage in editing your own writing is to achieve correctness, or, to use some language of the writing business, to get your writing into "Standard Edited Written English" (SEWE). This expression reflects the fact that readers expect your writing to follow standard conventions of spelling, grammatical usage, and mechanics. In fact, readers not only expect accuracy; they are irritated and even outraged when they find errors in something they read.

To understand why people are so concerned about correctness, it is useful to review a little history. About six hundred years ago, when printing was becoming widespread, it was discovered that there was little unity or consistency in English spelling and punctuation. Folks pretty much spelled the way they thought words sounded (just as a young child does today in generating "creative" spellings like "fir" for "fire" or "alot" for "a lot"). Writers in those days threw in punctuation marks wherever they thought they might look good, and they Capitalized every Word they thought was

Important and needed to Attract the Reader's Attention. These wide variances in spelling and punctuation created nightmares for printers, who couldn't always tell what word was meant in a manuscript. Readers also found it difficult to understand the variations, particularly as printing reached audiences spread over wider and wider geographical distances. As a result, printers and dictionary makers adopted many of the conventions we observe today. Rules of spelling and punctuation change, slowly, and are even evolving today. (We suspect that "alot," for example, will become a standard spelling one of these days, simply because so many adults use it that way.) However, since some great dictionary makers like Samuel Johnson did their work in the eighteenth century, our spelling and mechanics have remained more or less stable.

Correct grammar has a different historical origin. The Standard English we use has its roots in the dialect spoken and written around London, England, about six hundred years ago. Because London was the center and power of social and financial life in England, people out in the country regarded it as prestigious to talk and write like Londoners, wanting to seem like sophisticated city folks, not country bumpkins. London English became standard, and it has been passed along, with modifications, to us today.

In America we have our own standard English, at which some British stick up their noses. If you listen to the national six o'clock news, you'll hear something called "Standard Broadcast English," and if you read national magazines and newspapers, you'll find them in "Standard Edited Written English." (You'll also find that SEWE is the dialect taught in your school grammar book.)

So why do people make such a big fuss about correctness? It's partly a matter of convenience. If you're reading along in a book and find a word mspld or a punctuation mark. in the wrong? place, your reading is slowed down. More important, however, is that people have come to regard the ability to use Standard English as a mark of education. The writer who misspells or uses bad grammar is regarded poorly by his or her readership, and readers take a curious delight in showing their own education by finding errors in other people's work.

It is important, therefore, to get your writing into SEWE. Of course some errors will invariably creep in. Sometimes the mistakes will just be "typos" (short for *typographical errors*), simpl mistaks in copying somthing down. (There are three typos in the previous line!) Other times you'll make errors because you don't know the rules (we learned how to spell "genealogy" only after someone pointed out to us that we had spelled it "geneology" through an entire report—we just didn't know how it was spelled).

If you make occasional mistakes, whether typos or out of lack of knowledge, most readers will forgive you, but if you make a great many errors (or if you write in sloppy, illegible penmanship as well), many readers will be quite critical, and some won't even finish reading your work. We frankly think that such a reaction to errors in language is rather silly, and that since the days of standard London English, people have paid too much attention to correctness in writing. Nevertheless, the fact remains that you need to be concerned with it.

You may be one of those people who has a good memory for the rules of correctness and can keep them in your head. You can remember, for example, that "*I* comes before *E* except after *C*" or that "recommend" has one *C* and two *M*s. You know that "subjects and verbs agree in number" and use that rule to change "he don't" to "he doesn't." (If those last terms are not familiar to you, don't worry about it. You probably haven't studied grammar yet. You'll get to it before long in school.)

Many people, including a great many accomplished writers, are not able to keep all that information and those rules in their heads and must refer regularly to reference books to check on rules of spelling, grammar, and punctuation. You'll need to work out some strategies that are successful for you, either following rules in your head, learning how to use the reference books, or discovering other sources of help.

As a final stage in editing, then, check your paper for correctness. Some writers call this "proofreading," though a more accurate term is "copy editing." Either term means checking the paper carefully for errors in spelling, punctuation, and usage. Here are some strategies that may help:

1. *Spelling.* If you're a spelling champ or a pretty good speller or a not bad at all speller, congratulations; you've probably got ten to twenty thousand words in your brain that allow you to spell correctly. From time to time you may have to look things up, but most of the time you can "proof" your paper by reading it slowly and carefully. (We proof our manuscripts by placing a ruler under each line and slowly sliding it down the page, which forces us to look at the spelling of every word.)

If you're not an outstanding speller (or if you're a good speller and have encountered a word that looks unfamiliar or "funny" to you), you'll need to get help. The simplest source of assistance is to ask another person, preferably a person who is also a reliable speller. If you can find somebody who knows how to spell the word, that's faster than looking things up. (In school, check with your teacher to see if asking for spelling help is allowed.) It's even a good idea to have a partner copy edit your paper, looking for spelling errors you may have missed.

If you can't get help from a friend (or if it isn't allowed), turn to a dictionary and try to find the word spelled correctly. As long as you know your alphabet and know the first two or three letters of the word, the dictionary will work well for you. However, some writers prefer to look up words first in what's called a "spelling demon list," a collection of words that many people find troublesome to spell. You'll find these lists at the back of some school textbooks and in some dictionaries. Ask your teacher to help you locate one if this sounds interesting to you. A spelling demon list is handy because it is compact and quick to use, less cumbersome than a dictionary.

If you are systematic, you can save yourself time in the long run by making your own spelling list in your journal, writing down words that you have spelled incorrectly in the past or words that you find confusing and have to look up all the time. This individualized list will probably be quite short (unless you're an awful speller), and is even quicker to use than a spelling demon list.

Don't take shortcuts when proofreading your paper for spelling errors.

Perhaps more than any other kind of mistake, incorrect spelling puts readers off and gets you a less-than-fair reading.

(If you're a bad speller, you can improve your spelling by learning to be a good proofreader. Gradually you will learn those words that have always given you difficulty. If you want additional improvement in your spelling, play a lot of "Scrabble" or "Boggle," or do a lot of crossword puzzles and word searches.)

2. *Punctuation and Capitalization.* There are fewer rules to remember here than with spelling, yet a great many young (and old) writers have difficulty keeping the rules in mind. When do you use hyphens? Where do commas go? What's a semicolon good for? What can you capitalize in the middle of a sentence? You've probably studied those rules in school, and that's the best place to learn them. However, you should also keep reference sources on your desk to help. You'll find, for example, that most dictionaries will also have an appendix at the back summarizing the rules of capitalization and punctuation, and you'll also find them in grammar and usage handbooks. A list of reference books we recommend for young writers is given in Figure 12.

If you'd like to become independent of those reference books, however, we again recommend that you keep lists of rules and problems in your journal so you can look them up when you need them. If you make an error in capitalization and someone points it out to you, copy it down in your journal, both the wrong and the right ways. Chances are you'll encounter that sort of problem again in your writing.

3. *Usage and Grammar.* This is the most difficult kind of accuracy for most writers to achieve. Many people tend to write as they talk, and if your spoken dialect is different from Standard Edited Written English, you may have some difficulties. Your school grammar book summarizes most of the important rules, and it can be helpful. There are other quick reference tools available, too. For instance, we use a reference book called *Look It Up* (see Figure 12), which is an alphabetical listing of troublesome usage and spelling items. If we're confused over whether to use *who* or *whom* in a sentence, we look up "who" in the book and the rules are given. The bottom

Figure 12 *Reference Books for the Young Author's Library*

Dictionaries and Word Guides

Peter Funk. *It Pays to Increase Your Word Power*. New York: Bantam, 1968.

David Guralnik, ed. *Webster's New World Pocket Dictionary*. New York: Simon and Schuster, 1977.

Norman Lewis. *Instant Word Power*. New York: Signet, 1982.

Sylvester Mawson. *Roget's Pocket Thesaurus*. New York: Pocket Books, 1946 and later editions.

New Century Vest-Pocket Dictionary. New York: New Century, 1975.

Jess Stein. *The Random House Rhyming Dictionary*. New York: Random House, 1960.

Punctuation Guides

Robert Brittain. *A Pocket Guide to Correct Punctuation*. New York: Barron's Educational Series, Inc., 1981.

Harry Shaw. *Punctuate It Right!* New York: Harper and Row, 1963.

Spelling Guides

Francis Griffith. *A Pocket Guide to Correct Spelling*. New York: Barron's Educational Series, 1982.

Misspeller's Dictionary. New York: Simon and Schuster, 1983.

Usage

Rudolf Flesch. *Look It Up*. New York: Harper & Row, 1977.

Harry Shaw. *Errors in English and How to Correct Them*. New York: Barnes and Noble, 1972.

Michael Temple. *A Pocket Guide to Correct English*. New York: Barron's Educational Series, 1978.

Miscellaneous

The New Webster's Desk Reference Library. Belair Publishing. (Contains six small reference books in a box: dictionary, student's guide, speller, thesaurus, medical and law reference guides.)

line here is for you to find a reference book that you like and learn to use it.

Also helpful in achieving correct usage will be conferences with friends, parents, and teachers. Sometimes you just can't find a rule in your reference book that covers the situation you're dealing with. At that time, outside help is absolutely necessary. Too, it's useful to swap papers with other young writers so you can read each other's work for usage errors. While you may be a whiz on *who-whom*, one of your pals may be the real expert on *sit-set* or *shall-will*. Share your knowledge and expertise.

Preparing Final Copy

We began this chapter by noting that some writers confuse "revising" with "preparing clean copy." You can see by now that much has to go into changing and revising a manuscript before it's ready for final copy. If you have revised thoroughly and well, and if you have copy edited your manuscript carefully for mechanics, grammar, spelling, and capitalization, making a clean copy is relatively easy, requiring penmanship skills rather than brainpower.

Just make your copy as attractive as possible. Use your best penmanship and, if appropriate, write in an attractive color ink on attractive paper. If you know how to do calligraphy (formal, decorative penmanship) you might want to use that. In *Gifts of Writing* (Charles Scribner's Sons, 1980), we've shown a number of techniques you can use to make your final copy more attractive than usual. Our motto there was, "Make your writing look as good as it reads."

If at all possible, use a typewriter for final copy. We use the typewriter at all phases of the writing process, from making notes through drafting to preparing final copy. Learning to type was one of the most useful skills we ever acquired. If you're going to do a lot of writing in your life (which seems probable), you'll find typing an invaluable skill. As a fringe benefit to learning to type, some studies show that teachers grade typed papers higher than handwritten ones. Learning to type seems worth the effort.

ON THE JOYS OF WORD PROCESSORS

As you probably know, "word processors" are computers that let you draft on a television screen rather than on paper. A word processor allows you to do many of the revising jobs described by Jonathan Swift--blotting, refining, enlarging, deleting--electronically, at the touch of a button. With a word processor, you can "fiddle and faddle" to your heart's content, without having to make a clear copy each time. When you've finished and have the writing just the way you want it, you press a button and the printer spews out beautiful copy for you.

Part of this manuscript was written on a word processor, and it made our work go faster. However, word processing takes some getting used to, and there are some problems (like the time we pressed the wrong button and half this chapter disappeared into the electronic innards of the computer). The word processor is probably the typewriter of the future. In your lifetime, computers will become smaller and smaller, so that you may carry around a word processor just the way people carry electronic calculators today.

Even now you can probably get to use a word processor if you want to. Most schools have computers, and if you talk to the right people, they will let you do some writing on the word processor. Some experts even predict it will not be long before every school classroom has a computer/word processor available for its students.

However, as Herbert Philbrick, a freelance writer, has observed,

> Typing made easy with personal computers
> is not writing.*

There is no substitute for careful planning and revising a paper, and we hope this chapter has helped you see there is no substitute for careful editing, either.

---

*Herbert Philbrick, "The Writer's Life," *Writer's Digest* (December 1982).

Figure 13

Publishing Your Writing

10

Much of the writing you do is for your own satisfaction, and you may have little desire to show it to a wider audience. However, as you write more and feel more accomplished as a writer, you might enjoy sharing what you have written with family, friends, even people you don't know. This means "publishing" your writing, or "making it public." You can publish writing as simply as typing it and hanging it on a bulletin board; you can publish multiple copies on a mimeograph machine; or you might achieve the goal of most writers, having your work published in a newspaper, magazine, or even as a volume of your own.

Publishing for Family and Friends

Initially, your audience will probably be your family. Parents proudly display the work their children do, starting with the first handprint done in nursery school. Perhaps you have a bulletin board at home where messages of importance are left for the whole family to read. That might be a good place to post a poem or story or article you've written. Leaving it there where people can read it on their own avoids the situation where you must watch the person's expression while he or she reads or ask the inevitable question, "What didja think?" when they're done. If you feel comfortable doing so, leave a blank sheet of paper next to your writing for people to jot down comments and suggestions.

Think of other ways you can share with members of your family: If you have a younger brother or sister, perhaps you have written something you can read for their bedtime story. You might tape record some of your writing for other members of the family to listen to at their leisure. If other family members are interested in writing, any member of the group who has written something recently might read it at the dinner table.

Good friends are also good audiences to start with because they like—or, at least, accept—almost everything you do. Make an extra copy of something you are writing and give it to your friend. Save nickels and dimes and run a half dozen photocopies of your most recent work and distribute those to cronies at school. Spend time with fellow writers at school lunch, with members of the group sharing their works in progress or their finished writing.

Relatives and pen pals far away also make good audiences. "Publish" your writing by putting it in an envelope and sending it halfway across the country. You might send a piece you've been working on for a long time, or you might send a draft of something and ask for their comments.

Write poems for people on birthdays and holidays and send those instead of commercial cards. Give your little brother a mystery story for his birthday. Write an article for your mother about a subject she's curious about—raising cacti, changing the oil in her car, stargazing. Send your grandparents some family character sketches for their anniversary. Do a review of a school play for a theater buff who's moved away from your town. You can find dozens, if not hundreds, of audiences for your writing among friends and relatives near and far.

Publishing also implies doing up your writing in some sort of bound, permanent form. If you have a longer piece of writing—such as a short story or article or a collection of poems—you might want to make a booklet, binding the pages together and fastening them with staples. You can create covers of cardboard or paper, decorated with felt-tip pens or pasted on gift wrap, fabric, or wallpaper. Visit your local printer to look for different colors and weights of papers to use for your text and the covers of your booklets. You might even want to look for a book on the ancient art of bookbinding at your library and learn how to make a real bound book.

If you don't want to make your own book, you can find prebound books of various shapes and sizes at a stationery store. Many of these books—filled with blank pages and with bright, attractive covers—will contain more pages than you can fill with a single piece of writing. Consider using one to give your parents an add-a-story book, where you enter some new writing at fixed intervals, say, every six months or every year, to give them a record of your growth as a writer and as a person.

You can publish your writing by putting on "writing shows" for friends and neighbors. Consider gathering your brothers and sisters or a group of friends to enact a play you've written in honor of a friend's birthday. Write skits, poems, stories, and even pageants to be performed at special family gatherings—Thanksgiving, the Fourth of July, your grandparents' anniversary. Turn a friend's short story into a "reader's theater" production by reading it aloud while other friends pantomime the actions of the story. Have poetry readings in your front yard.

Finally, as one of the people most interested in writing in your family, you might take responsibility for planning and organizing a family newsletter, published once a month or once a year. You can invite people to submit news items that you write or rewrite into a running record of what your family is doing. You can also include your own essays and imaginative writing in the newsletter, and you can print several or many copies using a photocopy machine.

School Publications

Perhaps you want a broader audience than family and friends. Consider submitting your work to your school paper. Some school papers are based solely on "news," including news features, feature articles, editorials, and letters. In some schools, the paper is done by the journalism class, and they might not accept outside submissions. Check with the editor or the advisor to see if they are interested in having you write. Perhaps you have written something to give as a sample of your writing. Once they agree to have you submit, make certain you get a good idea of what sort of writing they want. Ask about how long the piece should be, whether there are any special rules (such as not using "I" in stories), even how to type your final copy.

Many schools include literary writing as well as news in the newspaper. Some schools even have a separate literary magazine to publish plays, stories, and poems. Ask around to find the editor and ask him/her a few questions about submission procedures. Do they want the manuscript typed or can it be handwritten? Single-spaced or double-spaced? Is there a maximum length? Make certain you know the due dates for submission of manuscripts.

If your school doesn't have a source for you to publish your writing, talk with some of your teachers about starting a publication. (Remember that in Chapter Five we suggested a hypothetical situation in which you could use letters to persuade the principal to start a school literary magazine.) To make a stronger case, gather your friends who are also interested in writing to show that there are a number of people involved.

If you are not successful in getting a new schoolwide publication started, try to convince your English teacher to have a *class* publication. Volunteer to be the editor and to take charge of handling the organizational work, so the teacher doesn't have to take on the extra burden. If you decide you want to start your own publication, be aware of the amount of work involved. Here are some of the tasks you will need to perform:

It's probably a good idea to establish an *editorial board*, a group of people who decide the format of the publication, the criteria for selecting pieces, and the actual writing to be included. They will probably be the people who do most of the work in preparing the publication. If your publication represents the whole school, you may have a teacher/advisor to help you make the more difficult decisions.

Your editorial board will need to establish a *budget* for the publication, and that involves doing some research into printing costs. Spirit duplicating (ditto) and mimeograph are cheapest and can generally be done at the school at no extra cost. Offset printing is more expensive and often involves a commercial printer, though it may be that your school district's vocational center can print your publication quite inexpensively as part of a class project. Early in the game you'll need to determine just how long your publication will be, which influences how many manuscripts you accept.

Next, establish your *editorial policy*. What kind of writing do you want to include? Do you want strictly imaginative or creative writing, or can students submit nonfiction articles as well? From whom will you accept submissions: just your English class? the whole school? the eighth grade only? You may want to establish rigid or suggested lengths for manuscripts, probably keeping the length on the short side so you can publish as many different pieces as possible, given the overall length of the publication.

You will need to develop a written statement that lets prospective contributors know the criteria you will use in choosing writing. Are you looking for writing that is primarily light and humorous? Do you want experimental writing or more conventional stuff? Do you want all kinds of fiction, or will you specialize, say, in science fiction, mysteries, or romance? Are there types of writing you *won't* accept? Explain how manuscripts will be selected. Does every member of the editorial board read every manuscript? Is there some sort of "point system" or rating scale involved?

Once the manuscripts have come in, the work has just begun. Among the tasks you may want to assign to individuals or subcommittees of the editorial board are:

—Editing or suggesting changes in manuscripts.

—Copy editing for correctness.

—Communicating with contributors to tell them their work has been accepted (or needs to be revised before publication).

—Typewriting or typesetting.

—Proofreading the printing masters or stencils.

—Running the mimeograph or ditto machine.

—Assembling and stapling the printed pages.

—Arranging for distribution around the school.

Much work. Much satisfaction when your first (and subsequent) issues "hit the stands."

Other Audiences

If you want an even larger audience than that provided by family and schoolmates, look into local publications that accept submissions from community members. For example, your local newspaper may have a section devoted to young people's writing. Some newspapers want student correspondents to write articles on school news and events. If your paper doesn't have anything like that now, you might write the editor to see if the paper would be interested in beginning a section given over to young writers.

Some communities have writing contests sponsored by the newspaper, arts organizations, historical societies, or public service groups. These are often announced through your local paper.

In Figure 14 we have listed some publications and writing contests at the national level that are open to young people. There are always new contests and publications coming into existence, frequently announced in the magazines that you read regularly. *Writer's Digest* and *The Writer* magazine also have monthly columns listing new contests and other publishing opportunities. *Writer's Market*, a book you will find at the library, also contains lists of writing contests.

When you are preparing a manuscript for a national publication (or a local one, for that matter), keep in mind that the publication is usually looking for a very specific type of writing. It is important to be well acquainted with the publication, to know what its purpose is, and to have a clear understanding of the kinds of writing it uses. Read a copy or two carefully, and look for editorial statements from the editor describing what he or she wants. Many publications will send you a description of publication guidelines if you send them a self-addressed, stamped envelope.

Remember that national magazines get thousands of submissions every

Figure 14 *Contests and Publications Open to Young Writers*

CONTESTS

National Achievement in Writing Awards (National Council of Teachers of English, 1111 Kenyon Road, Urbana, IL 61801). Essay-writing awards given to senior high school students.

The Cricket Magazine for Children (Cricket League, Box 100, LaSalle, IL 61301). Story-writing contests for age thirteen and under.

Elias Lieberman Student Poetry Award (Poetry Society of America, 15 Gramercy Park, New York, NY 10003). $100 awards given to high school students.

Guideposts Magazine Youth Writing Contest (Guideposts Associates, Inc., 747 Third Avenue, New York, NY 10017). For high school juniors and seniors. Scholarships of $1000–$4000 given for best personal experience stories.

PUBLICATIONS

Alive for Young Teens (Christian Board of Publication, Box 179, St. Louis, MO 63166). Publishes fiction, nonfiction, poetry, puzzles, riddles, tongue-twisters, daffy-nitions by twelve to fifteen year olds.

All American High School Magazine (Box 254800, Sacramento, CA 95865). Wants fiction from high school students.

Boy's Life Magazine (1325 Walnut Hill Lane, Irving, TX 75062). Readers' page for interesting ideas and a column on hobby projects.

Christian Living for Senior Highs (David C. Cook Publishing Company, 850 N. Grove, Elgin, IL 60120). Encourages submission of fiction and nonfiction for teenagers.

Highwire Magazine, National Student Magazine (Community Publishing Services, Box 948, 217 Jackson Street, Lowell, MA 01853). Publishes fiction, nonfiction, and fillers for high school students.

Jack and Jill (P.O. Box 567, Indianapolis, IN 46206). Stories, poems, riddles, and jokes written by children are considered.

Just About Me (JAM) (Ensio Industries, 247 Marlee Avenue, Suite 206, Toronto, Ontario, Canada M6B 4B8). A magazine for girls; accepts fiction and poetry from girls twelve to nineteen.

Probe (Baptist Brotherhood Commission, 1548 Poplar Avenue, Memphis, TN 38104). Wants personal experience stories by teenage boys from twelve to seventeen.

Purple Cow: Atlanta's Magazine for Kids (110 E. Andrews Drive NW, Atlanta, GA 30305). Publishes fiction and fillers for twelve to eighteen year olds.

Ranger Rick (1412 16th Street NW, Washington, DC 20036). Includes fiction, nonfiction, puzzles for children on nature/ecology theme.

Seventeen (850 Third Avenue, New York, NY 10022). Nonfiction, fiction, poetry by teens; also includes a teen-written column, "Free for All," with profiles, essays, expose, reportage, book reviews, and puzzles.

The Sunshine News (Canada Sunshine Publishing, Ltd., 465 King Street East #14A, Toronto, Ontario, Canada M5A 1L6). A "participation magazine" for high school students.

Young Ambassador (Good News Broadcasting Association, Inc., Box 82808, Lincoln, NE 68501). Wants short fillers from twelve to sixteen year olds.

year and that they can only publish a few. Don't be dismayed or quit if your writings aren't accepted immediately. Some writers have sent in writing for years before being published, and they have stacks of rejection letters that they display with a curious sort of pride. You'll probably collect a number of rejection slips before breaking into print.

Self-Publishing

If the grind and frustration of sending your writing around gets to be too much, or if you want to try a form of publication in which you are your own boss, try self-publishing. Create multiple copies of a single piece or do a collection of your works to sell.

Just as with a new school publication, you'll need to do some research into printing methods and costs before launching a self-publishing venture. Find out where you can get things printed at low cost and work up a budget.

At an early stage, think about ways of distributing your self-published work. You can get subscribers (people who will agree in advance to buy your work) or make plans to sell single copies once you've completed your work. It may be possible for you to distribute your publication around school, church, the YMCA, or your youth club. Some self-published writers advertise through classified ads in the local paper, or through fliers and posters distributed around the neighborhood. Like starting your own school magazine, self-publishing is time consuming and a lot of work, but it is also an extremely satisfying way to increase the audience for your work.

Index

Place and time to write, 14
Places, writing about, 45
Planning, 54
Plays, 86
Plot, 78
Poems, 91
Pope, Alexander, 126
Practical letters, 69
Precis, 103
Primitive writing, 2
Publicity, writing for, 72
Publishing, 144
Punctuation, 140
Puns, 37
Purpose, 49

Q

Questions, asking, 48; web, 110
Quotations, 38

R

Radio, writing to stations, 70; writing
    about, 40
Read, Herbert, 95
Records, writing about, 47
Reference books, 18; writers'
    bookshelf, 141
Reports, 107
Research, 111, 122
Resources, for school reports, 109, 111,
    122
Revising, 133
Riddles, 37
Rodgers, Dianne, 134
Roren, Ned, 42
Rosetti, Christina, 95

S

School publications, 146
School writing, 98
Science fiction, 84
Self-publishing, 152
Sensory writing, 32
Spelling, 139
Spender, Stephen, 62
Spikol, Art, 130
Stafford, Jean, 100
Stage directions, 89
Standard Edited Written English, 136
Stuart, Jesse, 60
Study questions, 105
Summary, 103
Swift, Jonathan, 40, 127

T

Television, writing to stations, 70;
    writing about, 41
Time and place to write, 14
Tools for writing, 16, 143
Topics, report, 107
Typing, 17, 142

U

Unblocking, 59
Uris, Leon, 20
Usage, 140
Uses of writing, 6

W

Web, question, 110
Wersba, Barbara, 8, 13, 58, 98